Tighe Surname

Ireland: 1600s to 1900s

From Ireland Church Records of Baptism, Marriage and Death

Comprised of Roman Catholic and Church of Ireland Records

From Counties Carlow, Cork, Kerry and Dublin City

Compiled by **Donovan Hurst**

December 1, 2012

Dedication

This work is dedicated to all of those that came before us and shaped our lives to make us the people that we are today.

Table of Contents

Introduction

This is a compilation of individuals who have the surname of Tighe that lived in the country of Ireland from the 1600s to the 1900s. I have placed each entry into one of four categories: Families, Individual Births/Baptisms, Individual Burials, and Individual Marriages. If a marriage entry primarily concerns an Individual Tighe whom is female, then I have placed that entry under the category of Individual Marriages. If a marriage entry primarily concerns an Individual Tighe whom is male, then I have placed that entry under the category of Families. Images of many of these listings are available at http://churchrecords.irishgenealogy.ie/churchrecords/.

To help guide the reader of this work, the format of this book is as follows:

- Main Family Entry (Husband and Wife) (Father and Mother)

  - Child of Main Family Entry, including Spouse(s) when available

    - Grandchild of Main Family Entry, including Spouse(s) when available

      - Great-Grandchild of Main Family Entry, including Spouse(s) when available

(**Bolded Text**) following any entry includes any additional information such as Residence(s), Occupation(s), Signature(s), etc. when available.

Hurst

Some of the fonts used in this work symbolizes Celtic writing. The traditional letters, numbers, and punctuation marks and their Celtic counterparts are as follows:

Traditional Letters (Uppercase & Lowercase)

A a B b C c D d E f G g H h I i J j K k L l M m N n O o P p Q q R r S s T t U u V v W w X x Y y Z z

Celtic Letters (Uppercase & Lowercase)

A a B b C c D ð E e F ƒ G g H h I í J j K k L l M m

N n O o P p Q q R ʀ S s T t U u V ʋ W ω X x Y y Z z

Traditional Numbers

1 2 3 4 5 6 7 8 9 10

Celtic Numbers

1 2 3 4 5 6 7 8 9 10

Traditional Punctuation

. , : ' " & - ( )

Celtic Punctuation

. , : ' " & - ( )

Parish Churches

Cork & Ross

(Roman Catholic or RC)

Bantry Parish, Clonakilty Parish, Cork - South Parish, Drimoleague Parish, and Rossalettiri & Kilkeraunmor (Roscarbery & Lissevard) Parish.

Dublin (Church of Ireland)

Arbour Hill Barracks Parish, Clondalkin Parish, Clontarf Parish, Glasnevin Parish, St. Andrew Parish, St. Anne Parish, St. Audoen Parish, St. Catherine Parish, St. George Parish, St. James Parish, St. Luke Parish, St. Mark Parish, St. Mary Parish, St. Michael Parish, St. Michan Parish, St. Nicholas Within Parish, St. Nicholas Without Parish, St. Patrick Parish, St. Paul Parish, St. Peter Parish, St. Stephen Parish, St. Thomas Parish, St. Werburgh Parish, and Taney Parish.

Dublin (Roman Catholic or RC)

Chapelizod Parish, Clondalkin Parish, Harrington Street Parish, Lucan Parish, Rathfarnham Parish, Rathmines Parish, Saggart Parish, Sandyford Parish, SS. Michael & John Parish, St. Agatha Parish, St. Andrew Parish, St. Audoen Parish, St. Catherine Parish, St. James Parish, St. Joseph Parish, St. Lawrence Parish, St. Mary Parish, St. Mary, Donnybrook Parish, St. Mary, Haddington Road Parish, St. Mary, Pro Cathedral Parish, St. Michan Parish, and St. Nicholas Parish.

Kerry (Church of Ireland)

Tralee Parish.

Kerry (Roman Catholic or RC)

Allihies Parish, Caherciveen Parish, Lixnaw Parish, and Tralee Parish.

$\mathbb{F}$amilies

- Anthony Tighe & Ellen Tighe

  - Ellen Tighe – bapt. 25 Sep 1833 (Baptism, **St. Mary, Pro Cathedral Parish** (RC))

- Barnabas (B a r n a b a s) Tighe & Cecelia Tighe, bur. 26 Jun 1755 (Burial, **St. Michael Parish**)

  - Daniel Tighe – bapt. 5 Oct 1750 (Baptism, **St. Michael Parish**)

  - Anne Tighe – bapt. 2 Jan 1753 (Baptism, **St. Michael Parish**)

  - Anne Tighe – bapt. 6 Mar 1754 (Baptism, **St. Michael Parish**)

- Bartholomew Tighe & Bridget O'Maily

  - Patrick Tighe – bapt. 10 Jan 1791 (Baptism, **St. Michan Parish** (RC))

- Bartholomew Tighe & Mary Fitzsimmons – 15 Dec 1782 (Marriage, **St. Michan Parish** (RC))

  - Catherine Tighe – bapt. 9 Nov 1783 (Baptism, **St. Michan Parish** (RC))

  - James Tighe – bapt. 5 Feb 1786 (Baptism, **St. Michan Parish** (RC))

- Bartholomew Tighe & Mary Nolan – 29 Jan 1826 (Marriage, **SS. Michael & John Parish** (RC))

- Bernard (B e r n a r d) Tighe & Elizabeth Unknown

  - John Tighe & Mary Dunne – 23 Sep 1860 (Marriage, **St. Catherine Parish** (RC))

John Tighe (son):

   Residence - 32 Meath Street - September 23, 1860

Mary Dunne, daughter of Hugh Dunne & Judith Unknown (daughter-in-law):

   Residence - 4 Pimlico - September 23, 1860

Hurst

- Bernard (B e r n a r d) Tighe & Mary Unknown

  - John Joseph Tighe – bapt. 1839 (Baptism, **St. Andrew Parish** (RC))

  - Bridget Tighe – bapt. 1841 (Baptism, **St. Andrew Parish** (RC))

  - Mary A. Tighe – bapt. Jul 1845 (Baptism, **SS. Michael & John Parish** (RC))

  - Michael Tighe – bapt. Jun 1850 (Baptism, **SS. Michael & John Parish** (RC))

- Bryan Tighe & Mary Conway – 21 Dec 1834 (Marriage, **St. Andrew Parish** (RC))

- Charles Tighe & Catherine Kelly

  - Bridget Tighe & John Cunningham – 21 Aug 1881 (Marriage, **St. Nicholas Parish** (RC))

Bridget Tighe (daughter):

    Residence - 51 New Street - August 21, 1881

John Cunningham, son of James Cunningham & Winifred Burke (son-in-law):

    Residence - 29 Queen Street - August 21, 1881

- Christopher Tighe & Mary Palmer

  - Jane Tighe – bapt. 10 Mar 1811 (Baptism, **SS. Michael & John Parish** (RC))

- Christopher Tighe & Mary Tighe

  - Mary Anne Tighe – bapt. 9 Dec 1804 (Baptism, **St. Mark Parish**)

- Christopher Tighe & Rose Meaghan

  - Christopher Tighe – bapt. 1826 (Baptism, **Lucan Parish** (RC))

- Christopher W. Tighe & Bridget Falkner

  - Patrick Joseph Tighe – b. 21 Jun 1904, bapt. 6 Jul 1904 (Baptism, **Rathmines Parish** (RC))

Christopher W. Tighe (father):

    Residence - St. Stephen Hospital - July 6, 1904

Tighe Surname Ireland: 1600s to 1900s

- Cornelius (C o r n e l i u s) Tighe & Anastasia Unknown

  o Bridget Tighe – bapt. 27 Jan 1788 (Baptism, **St. Nicholas Parish** (RC))

- Cornelius (C o r n e l i u s) Tighe & Elizabeth Connorty

  o Patrick Tighe – bapt. 24 Feb 1816 (Baptism, **St. James Parish** (RC))

- Cornelius (C o r n e l i u s) Tighe & Ellen Kellehan

  o Margaret Tighe – bapt. 20 Nov 1842 (Baptism, **Drimoleague Parish** (RC))

- Cornelius (C o r n e l i u s) Tighe & Ellen Kingston

  o John Tighe – bapt. 11 Sep 1843 (Baptism, **Drimoleague Parish** (RC))

- Cornelius (C o r n e l i u s) Tighe & Mary Unknown

  o Anne Tighe – bapt. 1800 (Baptism, **St. Andrew Parish** (RC))

- Cornelius (C o r n e l i u s) Tighe & Unknown

  o Catherine Tighe & John Fahey – 30 Oct 1870 (Marriage, **St. James Parish** (RC))

Catherine Tighe (daughter):

Residence - Kevin Street - October 30, 1870

John Fahey, son of Edward Fahey (son-in-law):

Residence - 16 Kevin Street - October 30, 1870

- Daniel Tighe & Ellen Brien

  o Margaret Tighe – bapt. 4 Jun 1848 (Baptism, **Drimoleague Parish** (RC))

- Daniel Tighe & Frances Tighe

  o Frederick Edward Tighe – b. 16 Jun 1826, bapt. 7 Aug 1826 (Baptism, **St. George Parish**)

- Daniel Tighe & Honor Corkery

  o Daniel Tighe – b. 8 May 1841, bapt. 8 May 1841 (Baptism, **Allihies Parish** (RC))

Hurst

Daniel Tighe (father):

Residence - Barnis - May 8, 1841

- Daniel Tighe & Julianne Mahony
  - Honor Tighe – bapt. 6 Nov 1836 (Baptism, **Drimoleague Parish** (RC))
- Dennis Tighe & Ellen Donovan
  - Dennis Tighe – bapt. 10 Mar 1844 (Baptism, **Drimoleague Parish** (RC))
- Dennis Tighe & Jane O'Byrne (O ' B y r n e)
  - James Tighe & Alice Foy – 15 May 1901 (Marriage, **St. Mary, Pro Cathedral Parish** (RC))

James Tighe (son):

Residence - 41 Amiens Street - May 15, 1901

Alice Foy, daughter of Peter Foy & Ellen Hunt (daughter-in-law):

Residence - 41 Amiens Street - May 15, 1901

- Dennis Tighe & Unknown
  - Winifred Tighe & Archibald Crichton – 17 Oct 1880 (Marriage, **St. Mary Parish**)

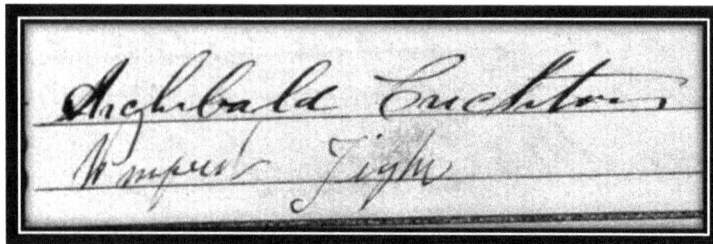

Signatures:

Winifred Tighe (daughter):

Residence - 21 Capel Street - October 17, 1880

Tighe Surname Ireland: 1600s to 1900s

Archibald Crichton, son of Archibald Crichton (son-in-law):

    Residence - 21 Capel Street - October 17, 1880

    Occupation - Watchmaker - October 17, 1880

    Relationship Status at Marriage - widow

Archibald Crichton (father):

    Occupation - Blacksmith

Dennis Tighe (father):

    Occupation - Shop Keeper

Wedding Witnesses:

Joseph Mitchell & Mary Robbins

Signatures:

- Dionysius Tighe & Jane O'Byrne (O ' B y r n e)

  - Mary Anne Tighe – b. 1 Mar 1873, bapt. 9 Mar 1873 (Baptism, **Rathmines Parish (RC)**)

  - Jane Charlotte Tighe – b. 18 Dec 1875, bapt. 21 Dec 1875 (Baptism, **St. James Parish (RC)**)

  - James Joseph Tighe – b. 26 Mar 1878, bapt. 1 Apr 1878 (Baptism, **St. Mary, Haddington Road Parish (RC)**)

Hurst

Dionysius Tighe (father):

Residence - Charlemont Street - March 9, 1873

Dolphin's Barn - December 21, 1875

3 South Lott's Road - April 1, 1878

- Edward Tighe & Bridget Clarke

  - John Tighe – b. 1833, bapt. 1833 (Baptism, Rathfarnham Parish (RC))

  - Robert Tighe – b. 1835, bapt. 1835 (Baptism, Rathfarnham Parish (RC))

  - Teresa Tighe – b. 1839, bapt. 1839 (Baptism, Rathfarnham Parish (RC))

  - Elizabeth Tighe – b. 1842, bapt. 1842 (Baptism, Rathfarnham Parish (RC))

  - Joseph Tighe – b. 1845, bapt. 1845 (Baptism, Rathfarnham Parish (RC))

  - Edward Tighe, b. 1848, bapt. 1848 (Baptism, Rathfarnham Parish (RC)) & Agnes Duffy – 27 Jun 1870 (Marriage, Rathmines Parish (RC))

    - Mary Bridget Tighe – b. 29 Mar 1871, bapt. 2 Apr 1871 (Baptism, St. Joseph Parish (RC))

    - Agnes Mary Tighe – b. 18 Oct 1873, bapt. 22 Oct 1873 (Baptism, St. Joseph Parish (RC))

    - Magaret Mary Tighe – b. 10 Jul 1875, bapt. 14 Jul 1875 (Baptism, St. Joseph Parish (RC))

Edward Tighe (son):

Residence - Roundtown - June 27, 1870

April 2, 1871

October 22, 1873

Lower Roundtown - July 14, 1875

Tighe Surname Ireland: 1600s to 1900s

Agnes Duffy, daughter of Thomas Duffy & Mary Goodwin (daughter-in-law):

Residence - Rathmines - June 27, 1870

- Edward Tighe & Mary Byrne (B y r n e)
  - Edward Tighe – bapt. 15 Jun 1827 (Baptism, **SS. Michael & John Parish (RC)**)
- Edward Tighe & Mary Unknown
  - Mary Tighe – bapt. 1822 (Baptism, **St. Andrew Parish (RC)**)
- Eugene Tighe & Bridget Unknown
  - Eugene Tighe & Alice Greene – 21 May 1871 (Marriage, **St. Michan Parish (RC)**)

Eugene Tighe (son):

Residence - Lagore Ratoath - May 21, 1871

Alice Greene, daughter of Patrick Greene & Mary Anne Unknown

(daughter-in-law):

Residence - Mountjoy Prison, North Circular Road - May 21, 1871

Remarks - Alice Green is the sister of Catherine Greene, who married

Nicholas Tighe on May 23, 1862

- Francis Tighe & Catherine Fitzsimons
  - Gertrude Mary Tighe – b. 20 Aug 1882, bapt. 30 Aug 1882 (Baptism, **St. Michan Parish (RC)**)
  - Florence Tighe – b. 2 Mar 1886, bapt. 15 Mar 1886 (Baptism, **St. Michan Parish (RC)**)
  - Mary Tighe – b. 18 Feb 1888, bapt. 12 Mar 1888 (Baptism, **St. Mary, Pro Cathedral Parish (RC)**)

Hurst

Francis Tighe (father):

Residence - 32 Glengarriffe Parade - August 30, 1882

8 St. Patrick Road - March 15, 1886

31 Grenville Street - March 12, 1888

- Francis Tighe & Catherine Unknown
  - Mary Anne Tighe – bapt. 12 Mar 1807 (Baptism, **St. Mary, Pro Cathedral Parish (RC)**)

- Francis Tighe & Eleanor Rone – 22 May 1769 (Marriage, **St. Andrew Parish (RC)**)

- Francis Tighe & Elizabeth Byrne (B y r n e)
  - John Tighe – b. 23 Jan 1889, bapt. 25 Jan 1889 (Baptism, **St. Mary, Pro Cathedral Parish (RC)**)

  - Mary Anne Tighe – b. 17 Dec 1890, bapt. 19 Dec 1890 (Baptism, **St. Mary, Pro Cathedral Parish (RC)**)

  - Charles Tighe – b. 4 Jan 1893, bapt. 9 Jan 1893 (Baptism, **St. Mary, Pro Cathedral Parish (RC)**)

  - Thomas Tighe – b. 13 May 1895, bapt. 20 May 1895 (Baptism, **SS. Michael & John Parish (RC)**)

  - Elizabeth Frances Tighe – b. 23 Jun 1897, bapt. 28 Jun 1897 (Baptism, **St. Mary, Pro Cathedral Parish (RC)**)

  - Peter Tighe – b. 11 Oct 1899, bapt. 16 Oct 1899 (Baptism, **St. Mary, Pro Cathedral Parish (RC)**)

Francis Tighe (father):

Residence - 27 Summer Hill - January 25, 1889

Tighe Surname Ireland: 1600s to 1900s

14 Upper Abbey Street - December 19, 1890

33 Cumberland Street - January 9, 1893

30 Upper Mercer Street - May 20, 1895

29 North Great George's Street - June 28, 1897

3 Lower Gloucester Street - October 16, 1899

- Francis Tighe & Mary Dowling – Unclear (Marriage, **St. Andrew Parish (RC)**)
- George Tighe & Catherine Hennessy
  - Henry Tighe – b. 1875, bapt. 1875 (Baptism, **St. Andrew Parish (RC)**)

George Tighe (father):

Residence - 17 Upper Mercer Street - 1875

- Gulielmo Tighe & Catherine Unknown
  - Patrick Tighe & Margaret Brennan – 24 Aug 1879 (Marriage, **St. Mary, Pro Cathedral Parish (RC)**)

Patrick Tighe (son):

Residence - 3 James Lane - August 24, 1879

Margaret Brennan, daughter of James Brennan & Catherine Unknown

(daughter-in-law):

Residence - Summer Hill - August 24, 1879

Wedding Witnesses:

Gulielmo Tighe & Alice Lynch

Hurst

- Gulielmo Tighe & Elizabeth O'Brien

  - Patrick Tighe – b. 8 Nov 1887, bapt. 11 Nov 1887 (Baptism, **St. Audoen Parish** (RC))

Gulielmo Tighe (father):

Residence - 30 Usher's Quay - November 11, 1887

- Gulielmo Francis Tighe & Mary Jane Hanlon – Feb 1852 (Marriage, **St. Michan Parish** (RC))

  - John Francis Xavier Tighe – b. 29 Nov 1854, bapt. 11 Dec 1854 (Baptism, **St. Mary, Pro Cathedral Parish** (RC))

Gulielmo Francis Tighe (father):

Residence - 3 Henry Street - December 11, 1854

Wedding Witnesses:

Nicholas Farrell & Mary Hanlon

- Henry Tighe & Martha Tighe

  - Elizabeth Tighe – bapt. 23 Mar 1800 (Baptism, **St. Mary Parish**)

- Henry Tighe & Mary Rorke – 26 Feb 1775 (Marriage, **St. Michan Parish** (RC))

- Hugh Tighe & Catherine Maxwell

  - Mary Anne Tighe – bapt. 5 Mar 1801 (Baptism, **St. Catherine Parish** (RC))

  - Isabel Tighe – bapt. 15 Mar 1803 (Baptism, **St. Catherine Parish** (RC))

  - Joseph Tighe – bapt. 22 Apr 1804 (Baptism, **St. Catherine Parish** (RC))

- Hugh Tighe & Eleanor Flood

  - Anne Tighe – bapt. 13 Oct 1790 (Baptism, **St. Michan Parish** (RC))

Tighe Surname Ireland: 1600s to 1900s

- Hugh Tighe & Elizabeth Monks – 29 Jun 1806 (Baptism, **St. Andrew Parish** (RC))

  o Michael Tighe – bapt. 1 Oct 1808 (Baptism, **St. Catherine Parish** (RC))

  o James Tighe – bapt. 23 Sep 1810 (Baptism, **St. Catherine Parish** (RC))

  o Elizabeth Tighe – b. 21 Jun 1812, bapt. 24 Jun 1812 (Baptism, **St. Catherine Parish** (RC))

  o Hugh Tighe – bapt. 12 Oct 1813 (Baptism, **St. Catherine Parish** (RC))

  o Cecelia Tighe – bapt. 11 Jan 1819 (Baptism, **St. Catherine Parish** (RC))

- Hugh Tighe & Elizabeth Tighe

  o Hugh Tighe – bapt. 9 Jun 1783 (Baptism, **St. Mary Parish**)

- Hugh Tighe & Elizabeth Unknown

  o Hugh Tighe – bapt. 1 Jun 1840 (Baptism, **St. Audoen Parish** (RC))

- Hugh Tighe & Margaret Fitzpatrick – 26 Jan 1812 (Marriage, **St. Michan Parish** (RC))

Wedding Witnesses:

John Kenning & Elizabeth Tighe

- Hugh Tighe & Margaret Unknown

  o Thomas Tighe – bapt. 1818 (Baptism, **St. Andrew Parish** (RC))

  o Mary Esther Tighe – bapt. 1820 (Baptism, **St. Andrew Parish** (RC))

  o Hugh Tighe – bapt. 1821 (Baptism, **St. Andrew Parish** (RC))

  o James Tighe – bapt. 1824 (Baptism, **St. Andrew Parish** (RC))

  o John Tighe – bapt. 1829 (Baptism, **St. Andrew Parish** (RC))

  o Catherine Tighe – bapt. 1831 (Baptism, **St. Andrew Parish** (RC))

- Hugh Tighe & Margaret Unknown

  o James Tighe & Elizabeth Mahony – 9 Jan 1876 (Marriage, **St. Mary, Pro Cathedral Parish** (RC))

Hurst

- Margaret Anne Tighe – b. 25 Jul 1877, bapt. 30 Jul 1877 (Baptism, **St. Mary, Pro Cathedral Parish** (RC))

James Tighe (son):

Residence - 45 Prussia Street - January 9, 1876

7 Granby Lane - July 30, 1877

Elizabeth Mahony, daughter of Christopher Mahony & Mary Anne Unknown

(daughter-in-law):

Residence - 7 Granby Lane - January 9, 1876

- Hugh Tighe & Margaret Anne Dunne – 13 Feb 1839 (Marriage, **St. Audoen Parish** (RC))
  - Thomas Tighe – bapt. May 1838 (Baptism, **St. Audoen Parish** (RC))
  - James Tighe – bapt. 24 May 1840 (Baptism, **St. Audoen Parish** (RC))
  - Catherine Tighe – bapt. Dec 1843 (Baptism, **St. Michan Parish** (RC))
  - Elizabeth Tighe – bapt. 4 May 1846 (Baptism, **St. Michan Parish** (RC))
  - Hugh Tighe – b. 16 Aug 1855, bapt. 26 Aug 1855 (Baptism, **St. Michan Parish** (RC))
  - Margaret Tighe – b. 20 Nov 1857, bapt. 29 Nov 1857 (Baptism, **St. Michan Parish** (RC))
  - Michael Tighe – b. 6 Dec 1858, bapt. 12 Dec 1858 (Baptism, **St. Michan Parish** (RC))
  - Michael Patrick Tighe – b. 12 Mar 1862, bapt. 14 Mar 1862 (Baptism, **St. Audoen Parish** (RC))

Hugh Tighe (father):

Residence - 52 Pill Lane - August 26, 1855

November 29, 1857

December 12, 1858

18 Usher's Street - March 14, 1862

- Hugh Tighe & Mary Ann Farrell – 6 May 1833 (Marriage, **SS. Michael & John Parish** (RC))
- Hugh Tighe & Unknown
  - William Tighe & Harriet Burriss Lloyd – 25 May 1874 (Marriage, **St. Peter Parish**)

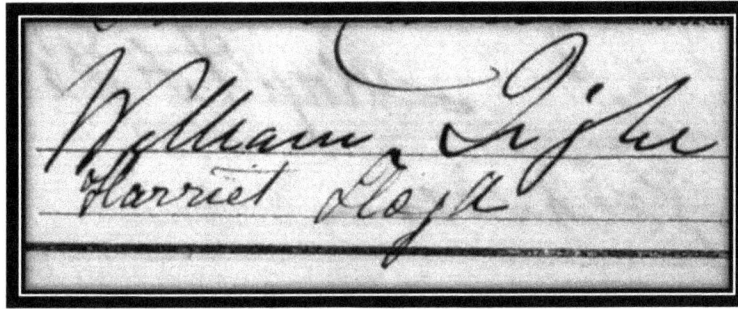

Signatures:

William Tighe (son):

Residence - 30 Merrion Square North - May 25, 1874

Occupation - Butler - May 25, 1874

Harriet Burris Lloyd, daughter of William Burriss (daughter-in-law):

Residence - Bellish Roserea - May 25, 1874

Relationship Status at Marriage - widow

William Burriss (father):

Occupation - Painter

Hugh Tighe (father):

Occupation - Butler

Hurst

Wedding Witnesses:

William Johnston & William Failrothe

Signatures:

- Hugh Ussher Tighe & Unknown

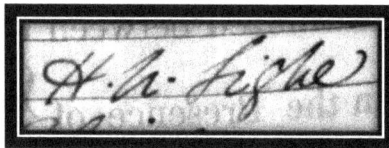

Signatures:

- Elizabeth Leticia Morgan Tighe & Edward James Stopford Blair – 22 Jun 1853 (Marriage, **St. Werburgh Parish**)

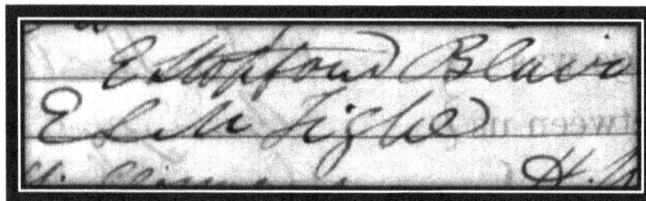

Signatures:

Tighe Surname Ireland: 1600s to 1900s

Elizabeth Leticia Morgan Tighe (daughter):

    Residence - Dublin Castle - June 22, 1853

    Occupation - Lady - June 22, 1853

Edward James Stopford Blair, son of William Henry Stopford Blair (son-in-law):

    Residence - Sackville Street, Dublin - June 22, 1853

    Occupation - Lieutenant H M 13th Light Dragoons - June 22, 1853

Thomas Henry Stopford Blair (father):

Signatures:

    Occupation - Lieutenant Colonel Royal Artillery

Hugh Ussher Tighe (father):

    Occupation - Dean of Leighlin

Hurst

Wedding Witnesses:

Hugh Ussher Tighe & William Henry Stopford Blair

Signatures:

- Catherine Florence Morgan Tighe & John Edward Severne (S e v e r n e) – 6 Jul 1858

  (Marriage, **St. Werburgh Parish**)

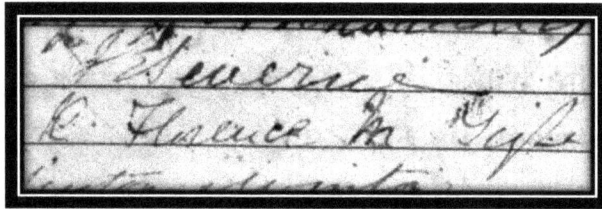

Signatures:

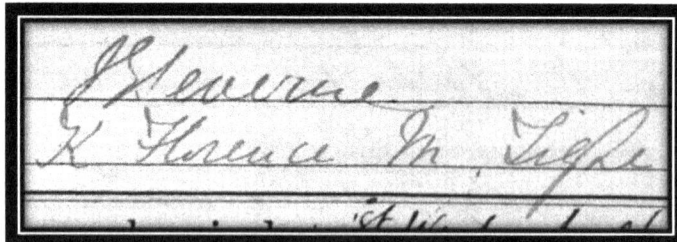

Catherine Florence Morgan Tighe (daughter):

Residence - Dublin Castle - July 6, 1858

Occupation - Daughter of a Clergyman - July 6, 1858

John Edward Severne, son of J. M. Severne (son-in-law):

Residence - Thenford Diocese of Peterborough, Northamptonshire -

July 6, 1858

Occupation - Gentleman, Esquire

J. M. Severne (father):

Occupation - Esquire

Hugh Ussher Tighe (father):

Occupation - Dean of Ardagh

Wedding Witnesses:

Eglinton Winton & E. Charles Severne

Signatures:

- James Tighe & Alice Ritchie

  o James Christopher Tighe – b. 20 Dec 1882, bapt. 4 Jan 1883 (Baptism, **SS. Michael & John Parish (RC)**)

Hurst

James Tighe (father):

Residence - 23 Temple Bar - January 4, 1883

- James Tighe & Anne Hackett
  - James Tighe, b. 19 Aug 1873, bapt. 2 Sep 1873 (Baptism, **St. James Parish** (RC)) & Margaret Cheevers – 5 Jul 1896 (Marriage, **Harrington Street Parish** (RC))
    - Joseph James Tighe – b. 10 Feb 1897, bapt. 11 Feb 1897 (Baptism, **SS. Michael & John Parish** (RC))
    - James Tighe – b. 1 Jul 1898, bapt. 4 Jul 1898 (Baptism, **SS. Michael & John Parish** (RC))
    - Jane Tighe – b. 4 Mar 1900, bapt. 6 Mar 1900 (Baptism, **Harrington Street Parish** (RC))

James Tighe (son):

Residence - 33 Nicholas Street - July 5, 1896

53 St. George's Street - February 11, 1897

July 4, 1898

3 Montague Place - March 6, 1900

Margaret Cheevers, daughter of Joseph Cheevers & Jane O'Rourke

(daughter-in-law):

Residence - 5 Montague Place - July 5, 1896

  - Mary Jane Tighe – b. 15 Jun 1878, bapt. 9 Jul 1878 (Baptism, **St. James Parish** (RC))
  - Margaret Tighe & John Flynn – 22 Apr 1895 (Marriage, **St. Mary, Donnybrook Parish** (RC))

Tighe Surname Ireland: 1600s to 1900s

- Mary Pauline Flynn – b. 28 Jun 1896, bapt. 5 Jul 1896 (Baptism, **Rathmines Parish (RC)**)

Margaret Tighe (daughter):

Residence - Brookvale, Donnybrook - April **22, 1895**

John Flynn, son of Simon Flynn & Mary Unknown (son-in-law):

Residence - 115 Guinness Buildings, Heytesbury Street, Dublin - April **22, 1895**

Portobello Barracks - July **5, 1896**

James Tighe (father):

Residence - 8 Old Kilmainham - September **2, 1873**

Inchicore - July **9, 1878**

- James Tighe & Anne Masterson
  - Joseph Tighe – bapt. Jul 1829 (Baptism, **St. Nicholas Parish** (RC))
  - Joseph Tighe – bapt. 26 Aug 1830 (Baptism, **St. Nicholas Parish** (RC))
- James Tighe & Anne Unknown
  - John Tighe – bapt. Dec 1836 (Baptism, **SS. Michael & John Parish** (RC))
  - John Tighe – bapt. Dec 1838 (Baptism, **SS. Michael & John Parish** (RC))
  - Mary Tighe – bapt. 1839 (Baptism, **St. Andrew Parish** (RC))
  - Patrick Tighe – bapt. 9 Nov 1841 (Baptism, **SS. Michael & John Parish** (RC))
- James Tighe & Anne Unknown
  - John Francis Tighe & Mary Brady – 23 Feb 1862 (Marriage, **St. Andrew Parish** (RC))
    - Anne Mary Tighe – b. 1868, bapt. 1868 (Baptism, **St. Andrew Parish** (RC))
    - Mary Anne Tighe – b. 1870, bapt. 1870 (Baptism, **St. Andrew Parish** (RC))
    - Francis James Tighe – b. 1874, bapt. 1874 (Baptism, **St. Andrew Parish** (RC))

- Patrick Joseph Tighe – b. 1874, bapt. 1874 (Baptism, **St. Andrew Parish** (RC))

- Ellen Tighe – b. 1875, bapt. 1875 (Baptism, **St. Andrew Parish** (RC))

John Francis Tighe (son):

Residence - 3 Burke Court, Pembroke Street - February 23, 1862

Burke's Court - 1868

3 Bourke's Court - 1870

4 Quinn's Lane - 1874

4 Bucks Court - 1875

Mary Brady, daughter of James Brady & Mary Unknown (daughter-in-law):

Residence - 4 Burke Court - February 23, 1862

- James Tighe & Anne Unknown
  - Joseph Tighe & Teresa Roche – 11 Jan 1867 (Marriage, **St. Mary, Pro Cathedral Parish** (RC))
    - Anne Mary Tighe – b. 29 Nov 1866, bapt. 29 Mar 1867 (Baptism, **St. Mary, Pro Cathedral Parish** (RC))
    - Joseph James Tighe – b. 9 Aug 1868, bapt. 19 Aug 1868 (Baptism, **St. Mary, Pro Cathedral Parish** (RC))
    - Peter John Tighe – b. 27 Jul 1870, bapt. 10 Aug 1870 (Baptism, **St. Mary, Pro Cathedral Parish** (RC))
    - Patrick Thomas Tighe – b. 26 Sep 1871, bapt. 6 Oct 1871 (Baptism, **St. Mary, Pro Cathedral Parish** (RC))

Tighe Surname Ireland: 1600s to 1900s

Joseph Tighe (son):

Residence - 52 Henry Street - January 11, 1867

March 29, 1867

61 Mary Street - August 19, 1868

7 Upper Abbey Street - August 10, 1870

28 Abbey Street - October 6, 1871

Teresa Roche, daughter of Thomas Roche & Catherine Unknown

(daughter-in-law):

Residence - 52 Henry Street - January 11, 1867

Wedding Witnesses:

Anne Roche & Edward Gurkin

- James Tighe & Catherine Doran

    o Martin Tighe – bapt. 1833 (Baptism, St. Mary Parish (RC))

    o Mary Tighe – bapt. 1839 (Baptism, St. Mary Parish (RC))

- James Tighe & Catherine Doyle

    o Owen Tighe – bapt. 1846 (Baptism, St. Mary Parish (RC))

- James Tighe & Catherine Murphy

    o Elizabeth Tighe – bapt. 1845 (Baptism, St. Mary Parish (RC))

- James Tighe & Catherine Tighe

    o Mary Anne Tighe – bapt. 30 Mar 1835 (Baptism, St. Mary, Pro Cathedral Parish (RC))

Hurst

- James Tighe & Catherine Unknown

  o Anne Tighe – bapt. 23 Sep 1819 (Baptism, **St. Mary, Pro Cathedral Parish** (RC))

Jams Tighe (father):

Residence - Proby's Lane - September 23, 1819

- James Tighe & Catherine Unknown

  o William Tighe – bapt. 1831 (Baptism, **St. Andrew Parish** (RC))

- James Tighe & Catherine Unknown

  o Owen Tighe & Clara Madden – 29 Aug 1869 (Marriage, **St. Andrew Parish** (RC))

    ▪ Catherine Tighe, b. 1870, bapt. 1870 (Baptism, **St. Mary Parish** (RC)) & Joseph Maloney

      – 28 Feb 1905 (Marriage, **St. Mary, Donnybrook Parish** (RC))

Catherine Tighe (daughter):

Residence - Eglinton Road - February 28, 1905

Joseph Maloney, son of Joseph Maloney & Mary Murray (son-in-law):

Residence - 8 Verschoyle Place - February 28, 1905

Wedding Witnesses:

John Maloney & Mary Coady

  ▪ William Tighe – b. 1872, bapt. 1872 (Baptism, **St. Mary Parish** (RC))

  ▪ James Tighe – b. 1875, bapt. 1875 (Baptism, **St. Mary Parish** (RC))

  ▪ John Patrick Tighe – b. 2 Mar 1877, bapt. 5 Mar 1877 (Baptism, **St. Mary, Haddington**

    Road Parish (RC))

Tighe Surname Ireland: 1600s to 1900s

- Michael Tighe – b. 29 Sep 1879, bapt. 29 Sep 1879 (Baptism, **St. Mary, Haddington Road Parish** (RC))

- Owen Tighe – b. 27 Sep 1882, bapt. 2 Oct 1882 (Baptism, **St. Mary, Haddington Road Parish** (RC))

Owen Tighe (son):

Residence - 9 Upper Baggot Street - August 29, 1869

24 Baggot Lane - March 5, 1877

October 2, 1882

12 Eastmoreland Place - September 29, 1879

Clara Madden, daughter of Timothy Madden & Esther Unknown (daughter-in-law):

Residence - 7 Brown's Cottages - August 29, 1869

- James Tighe & Catherine Unknown
  - James Tighe & Catherine McCormick (M c C o r m i c k) – 29 Oct 1871 (Marriage, **St. Andrew Parish** (RC))
    - James Tighe – b. 1872, bapt. 1872 (Baptism, **St. Mary Parish** (RC))

James Tighe (son):

Residence - 42 City Quay - October 29, 1871

Catherine McCormick, daughter of Christopher McCormick & Jane Unknown (daughter-in-law):

Residence - 52 Powers Court - October 29, 1871

Hurst

- James Tighe & Catherine Unknown

  - Thomas Henry Tighe & Kathleen Mary Freston – 27 Jan 1881 (Marriage, **St. Michan Parish (RC)**)

Thomas Henry Tighe (son):

Residence - Ballina - January 27, 1881

Kathleen Mary Freston, daughter of Luke Freston & Catherine Unknown

(daughter-in-law):

Residence - Peafiled Terrace, Black Rock - January 27, 1881

Wedding Witnesses:

Martin R. Hogan & Eleanor Freston

- James Tighe & Eleanor Unknown

  - Patrick Tighe – bapt. 1817 (Baptism, **St. Andrew Parish** (RC))

- James Tighe & Elizabeth Tighe

  - William Tighe – b. 17 Nov 1822, bapt. 1 Dec 1822 (Baptism, **St. George Parish**)

- James Tighe & Elizabeth Unknown

  - James Tighe – b. 8 Jan 1824, bapt. 25 Jan 1824 (Baptism, **St. Peter Parish**)

- James Tighe & Hannah Foster

  - James Tighe – b. 20 Jul 1857, bapt. 27 Jul 1857 (Baptism, **St. Michan Parish** (RC))

James Tighe (father):

Residence - 13 White's Lane - July 27, 1857

Tighe Surname Ireland: 1600s to 1900s

- James Tighe & Hannah Unknown

  o James Tighe & Mary Bradshaw – 3 Aug 1879 (Marriage, **St. Andrew Parish (RC)**)

James Tighe (son):

Residence - 161 Townsend Street - August 3, 1879

Mary Bradshaw, daughter of Hamilton Bradshaw & Elizabeth Unknown

(daughter-in-law):

Residence - 21 Anglesea Street - August 3, 1879

- James Tighe & Margaret O'Nateran – 8 Jun 1788 (Marriage, **St. Nicholas Parish (RC)**)
- James Tighe & Margaret Sullivan

  o Thomas Tighe – b. 19 Jul 1861, bapt. 19 Jul 1861 (Baptism, **Caherciveen Parish (RC)**)

James Tighe (father):

Residence - Caherciveen - July 19, 1861

- James Tighe & Martha Tighe

  o Henry Tighe – bapt. 16 Sep 1739 (Baptism, **St. Nicholas Within Parish**)

- James Tighe & Mary Carr

  o Anne Tighe – b. 1873, bapt. 1873 (Baptism, **St. Andrew Parish (RC)**)

James Tighe & Unknown

Residence - 16 Delany's Place - 1873

- James Tighe & Mary Martin – 3 Dec 1832 (Marriage, **Lucan Parish (RC)**)

  o Thomas Tighe – bapt. 1836 (Baptism, **Lucan Parish (RC)**)

Hurst

- ○ Edward Tighe – bapt. 1838 (Baptism, **Lucan Parish** (RC))

- ○ David Tighe – bapt. 1839 (Baptism, **Lucan Parish** (RC))

- ○ Catherine Tighe – bapt. 1840 (Baptism, **Lucan Parish** (RC))

- James Tighe & Mary McNerny (M c N e r n y) – 21 Aug 1811 (Marriage, **St. Andrew Parish** (RC))

- James Tighe & Mary Minnatur – 22 Nov 1803 (Marriage, **St. Andrew Parish** (RC))

- James Tighe & Mary Mullen

  - ○ Anne Mary Tighe – b. 3 Aug 1886, bapt. 14 Aug 1886 (Baptism, **St. Audoen Parish** (RC))

  - ○ Thomas Christopher Tighe – b. 30 Dec 1887, bapt. 3 Jan 1888 (Baptism, **St. Audoen Parish** (RC))

  - ○ Gulielmo Tighe – b. 20 Aug 1891, bapt. 25 Aug 1891 (Baptism, **St. Audoen Parish** (RC))

James Tighe (father):

Residence - 7 Christ Church Place - August 14, 1886

January 3, 1888

33 Nicholas Street - August 25, 1891

- James Tighe & Mary Tighe

  - ○ John Tighe – bapt. 6 Jun 1832 (Baptism, **St. Mary, Pro Cathedral Parish** (RC))

- James Tighe & Mary Tighe

  - ○ John Tighe & Mary Anne Saddlier – 26 Jun 1864 (Marriage, **Clondalkin Parish** (RC))

    - ▪ Mary Jane Tighe – b. 1866, bapt. 1866 (Baptism, **Clondalkin Parish** (RC))

    - ▪ Mary Tighe – b. 1871, bapt. 1871 (Baptism, **Clondalkin Parish** (RC))

Tighe Surname Ireland: 1600s to 1900s

John Tighe (son):

    Residence - Milltown - June 26, 1864

        Gallinstown - 1866

        Clondalkin - 1871

Mary Anne Saddler, daughter of Richard Saddlier & Mary Unknown

(daughter-in-law):

    Residence - 8th Lock - June 26, 1864

- Mary Anne Tighe & Simon Doyle – 17 Oct 1876 (Marriage, **Clondalkin Parish (RC)**)

Mary Anne Tighe (daughter):

    Residence - Milltown - October 17, 1876

Simon Doyle, son of Dennis Doyle & Sarah Unknown (son-in-law):

    Residence - Milltown - October 17, 1876

- James Tighe & Mary Unknown
  - Bartholomew Tighe – bapt. 4 Aug 1751 (Baptism, **St. Michan Parish (RC)**)
  - Bridget Tighe – bapt. 10 Feb 1760 (Baptism, **St. Michan Parish (RC)**)
- James Tighe & Mary Unknown
  - Margaret Tighe – bapt. 5 Apr 1819 (Baptism, **St. Mary, Pro Cathedral Parish (RC)**)
  - Mary Tighe – bapt. 8 Apr 1821 (Baptism, **St. Mary, Pro Cathedral Parish (RC)**)
  - Catherine Tighe – bapt. 6 Feb 1823 (Baptism, **St. Mary, Pro Cathedral Parish (RC)**)

James Tighe (father):

    Residence - Mad Island - February 6, 1823

Hurst

- James Tighe & Mary Unknown

    o Mary Tighe – bapt. 6 Mar 1835 (Baptism, **SS. Michael & John Parish (RC)**)

- James Tighe & Mary Anne Brean

    o Eleanor Tighe – bapt. 10 Mar 1822 (Baptism, **St. Michan Parish (RC)**)

- James Tighe & Mary Anne Unknown

    o James Tighe & Esther Healy – 1 Sep 1862 (Marriage, **St. Mary, Pro Cathedral Parish (RC)**)

    ▪ James Henry Joseph Tighe – b. 20 Oct 1863, bapt. 26 Oct 1863 (Baptism, **St. Mary, Pro Cathedral Parish (RC)**)

    ▪ John Michael Tighe – b. 15 Dec 1865, bapt. 20 Dec 1865 (Baptism, **St. Mary, Pro Cathedral Parish (RC)**)

    ▪ Peter Paul C. Tighe – b. 17 Dec 1867, bapt. 23 Dec 1867 (Baptism, **St. Mary, Pro Cathedral Parish (RC)**)

James Tighe (son):

Residence - 94 Upper Dorset Street - September 1, 1862

22 Lower Dorset Street - October 26, 1863

29 Lower Dorset Street - December 20, 1865

December 23, 1867

Esther Healy, daughter of John Healy & Mary Unknown (daughter-in-law):

Residence - 171 Great Britain Place - September 1, 1862

Wedding Witnesses:

Michael Dowling & Mary Healy

Tighe Surname Ireland: 1600s to 1900s

- James Tighe & Rose Meehan

  o Michael Tighe – bapt. 1832 (Baptism, **Clondalkin Parish (RC)**)

- James Tighe & Teresa Unknown

  o Unknown Anne Tighe – bapt. Jul 1840 (Baptism, **SS. Michael & John Parish** (RC))

- James Tighe & Unknown

  o William Henry Tighe & Catherine Rowan – 24 Jan 1853 (Marriage, **St. Mary Parish**)

Signatures:

William Henry Tighe (son):

    Residence - 33 Peter Street - January 24, 1853

    Occupation - Gentleman - January 24, 1853

Catherine Rowan, daughter of Joseph Rowan (daughter-in-law):

    Residence - 69 Upper Dominick Street - January 24, 1853

    Relationship Status at Marriage - minor age

Joseph Rowan (father):

    Occupation - Agent

James Tighe (father):

    Occupation - Musician

Hurst

Wedding Witnesses:

Edward Peter Duews & John Felton Leeds

Signatures:

- James Tighe & Unknown

  o John Michael Tighe & Edith Jane Pearson – 17 Aug 1894 (Marriage, **St. Audoen Parish**)

Signatures:

John Michael Tighe (son):

  Residence - 14 Anna Villa North Circular Road, Dublin - August 17, 1894

  Occupation - BA Candidate MB - August 17, 1894

Edith Jane Pearson, daughter of William Pearson (daughter-in-law):

  Residence - Synod House Christchurch Place - August 17, 1894

Tighe Surname Ireland: 1600s to 1900s

William Pearson (father):

Signature:

Occupation - Verger of Christchurch Cathedral

James Tighe (father):

Occupation - Pensioner in Civil Service

Wedding Witnesses:

William Pearson & M. Ganly

known, or if parties are unwilling to state them, a

Signatures:

- James Stuart Tighe & Unknown

  o Wilfred Tighe & Lucy Emily Lewin – 21 Apr 1898 (Marriage, **St. Stephen Parish**)

Signatures:

Hurst

Wilfred Tighe (son):

Residence - Rossanagh Ashford, Co. Wicklow - April 21, 1898

Occupation - Esquire - April 21, 1898

Lucy Emily Lewin, daughter of Frederick Thomas Lewin (daughter-in-law):

Residence - Castlegrove--- - April 21, 1898

Frederick Thomas Lewin (father):

Signature:

Occupation - Esquire

James Stuart Tighe (father):

Occupation - Colonel

Wedding Witnesses:

Marion Elizabeth Corrie & Frederick Thomas Lewin

Signatures:

- John Tighe & Alice Keely – 15 Oct 1849 (Marriage, **St. Catherine Parish (RC)**)

- John Tighe & Anne Doyle – 15 Feb 1819 (Marriage, **St. Mary, Pro Cathedral Parish (RC)**)

  o John Tighe – bapt. 24 Nov 1823 (Baptism, **St. Mary, Pro Cathedral Parish (RC)**)

Tighe Surname Ireland: 1600s to 1900s

John Tighe (father):

Residence - Dorset Street - November 24, 1823

- John Tighe & Anne Halpin

  o John Bernard (B e r n a r d) Tighe – b. 25 Feb 1857, bapt. 2 Mar 1857 (Baptism, **St. Mary, Pro Cathedral Parish** (RC))

John Tighe (father):

Residence - 10 Dorset Street - March 2, 1857

- John Tighe & Anne Hamilton

  o Patrick Tighe – b. 1875, bapt. 1875 (Baptism, **St. Andrew Parish** (RC))

  o Teresa Tighe – b. 1877, bapt. 1877 (Baptism, **St. Andrew Parish** (RC))

  o Ellen Tighe – b. 1880, bapt. 1880 (Baptism, **St. Andrew Parish** (RC))

John Tighe (father):

Residence - 55 Dawson Street - 1875

1880

55 Townsend Street - 1877

- John Tighe & Anne Tighe

  o Thomas Joseph Tighe – b. 14 Apr 1876, bapt. 2 May 1876 (Baptism, **St. James Parish** (RC))

John Tighe (father):

Residence - 1 James Street - May 2, 1876

Hurst

- John Tighe & Bridget McDonnell

  - Catherine Tighe – bapt. 11 Jul 1815 (Baptism, **SS. Michael & John Parish** (RC))

- John Tighe & Bridget Smith

  - Edward Tighe – bapt. 21 Feb 1837 (Baptism, **St. Catherine Parish** (RC))

- John Tighe & Catherine Carney (C a r n e y) – 1 Oct 1781 (Marriage, **St. Nicholas Parish** (RC))

  - James Tighe – bapt. 6 Jul 1792 (Baptism, **St. Catherine Parish** (RC))

- John Tighe & Catherine Considine

  - John A. Tighe – b. 22 Feb 1870, bapt. 13 Mar 1870 (Baptism, **Rathmines Parish** (RC))

  - Joseph Stephen Tighe – b. 26 Dec 1871, bapt. 20 Jan 1872 (Baptism, **Rathmines Parish** (RC))

John Tighe (father):

Residence - Rathgar - March 13, 1870

January 20, 1872

- John Tighe & Catherine Unknown

  - Margaret Tighe – bapt. 22 Jul 1786 (Baptism, **St. Nicholas Parish** (RC))

  - Christopher Tighe – bapt. 3 Jun 1789 (Baptism, **St. Nicholas Parish** (RC))

- John Tighe & Catherine Unknown

  - Hannah Tighe & James Stapleton – 12 Nov 1879 (Marriage, **St. Andrew Parish** (RC))

Hannah Tighe (daughter):

Residence - 161 Townsend Street - November 12, 1879

James Stapleton, son of John Stapleton & Mary Unknown (son-in-law):

Residence - 28 Queen's Street - November 12, 1879

- John Tighe & Catherine Wall

  - John Tighe – bapt. 30 Jan 1863 (Baptism, **St. Mary, Pro Cathedral Parish (RC)**)

John Tighe (father):

Residence - 65 Lower Mecklenburgh Street - January 30, 1863

- John Tighe & Eleanor Unknown

  - Elizabeth Tighe – bapt. 1808 (Baptism, **St. Andrew Parish (RC)**)

- John Tighe & Eleanor Unknown

  - Joseph Tighe & Margaret Donovan – 23 Feb 1876 (Marriage, **St. Catherine Parish (RC)**)

    - Mary Anne Tighe – b. 4 Oct 1876, bapt. Oct 1876 (Baptism, **St. Catherine Parish (RC)**)

    - Thomas Tighe – b. 4 Oct 1876, bapt. Oct 1876 (Baptism, **St. Catherine Parish (RC)**)

Joseph Tighe (son):

Residence - 63 Cork Street - February 23, 1876

Margaret Donovan, daughter of Thomas Donovan & Bridget Unknown

(daughter-in-law):

Residence - 35 New Row - February 23, 1876

- John Tighe & Eliya Grant – 24 Feb 1840 (Marriage, **St. Audoen Parish (RC)**)

Wedding Witnesses:

John Tighe & Margaret Tighe

- John Tighe & Elizabeth McDaniel

  - William Tighe – bapt. 17 Apr 1826 (Baptism, **SS. Michael & John Parish (RC)**)

Hurst

- John Tighe & Elizabeth Paris

  - Elizabeth Rosalie Tighe – b. 2 Sep 1875, bapt. 6 Sep 1875 (Baptism, **St. Mary, Pro Cathedral Parish** (RC))

John Tighe (father):

Residence - 4 Talbot Place - September 6, 1875

- John Tighe & Elizabeth Power

  - Gulielmo Joseph Tighe – b. 31 Aug 1859, bapt. 2 Sep 1859 (Baptism, **St. Mary, Pro Cathedral Parish** (RC))

  - James Tighe – b. 19 Jan 1861, bapt. 21 Jan 1861 (Baptism, **St. Mary, Pro Cathedral Parish** (RC))

  - Mary Anne Tighe – b. 13 Sep 1862, bapt. 15 Sep 1862 (Baptism, **St. Mary, Pro Cathedral Parish** (RC))

  - Catherine Tighe – b. 15 Nov 1864, bapt. 21 Nov 1864 (Baptism, **St. Mary, Pro Cathedral Parish** (RC))

  - Joseph Tighe, b. 1869, bapt. 1869 (Baptism, **St. Andrew Parish** (RC)) & Mary McDonagh – 23 May 1901 (Marriage, **St. Mary, Pro Cathedral Parish** (RC))

Joseph Tighe (son):

Residence - 15 Tara Street - May 23, 1901

Mary McDonagh, daughter of Patrick McDonagh & Elizabeth Hancock

(daughter-in-law):

Residence - 26 North Cumberland Street - May 23, 1901

Tíghe Surname Ireland: 1600s to 1900s

Wedding Witnesses:

John Tíghe & Catherine McDonagh

- o John Tighe – b. 13 Apr 1879, bapt. 16 Apr 1879 (Baptism, **St. Mary, Pro Cathedral Parish** (RC))

John Tíghe (father):

Residence - **198 Great Britain Street - September 2, 1859**

January 21, 1861

September 15, 1862

November 21, 1864

2 South Anne Street - 1869

4 Talbot Place - April 16, 1879

- John Tighe & Elizabeth Tighe
  - o Anne Tighe & Martin Gildea – 30 Apr 1865 (Marriage, **St. Mary, Pro Cathedral Parish** (RC))
    - Michael Patrick Gildea – b. 11 Jun 1866, bapt. 20 Jun 1866 (Baptism, **St. Mary, Pro Cathedral Parish** (RC))
    - Mary Elizabeth Gildea – b. 22 Oct 1869, bapt. 25 Oct 1869 (Baptism, **St. Mary, Pro Cathedral Parish** (RC))

Anne Tíghe (daughter):

Residence - **48 Montgomery Street - April 30, 1865**

Hurst

Martin Gildea, son of Martin Gildea & Anne Unknown (son-in-law):

Residence - 48 Montgomery Street - April 30, 1865

82 Great Britain Street - June 20, 1866

53 Montgomery Street - October 25, 1869

- John Tighe & Elizabeth Unknown
  - Mary Anne Tighe – bapt. 5 Sep 1836 (Baptism, **St. Mary, Pro Cathedral Parish (RC)**)
  - William Tighe – bapt. 5 Sep 1836 (Baptism, **St. Mary, Pro Cathedral Parish (RC)**)
  - Elizabeth Tighe – bapt. 1 Oct 1838 (Baptism, **St. Mary, Pro Cathedral Parish (RC)**)
- John Tighe & Elizabeth Unknown
  - Margaret Tighe & Michael Noonan – 26 Apr 1861 (Marriage, **St. Mary, Pro Cathedral Parish (RC)**)
    - Mary Ellen Noonan – b. 7 Nov 1861, bapt. 8 Nov 1861 (Baptism, **St. Nicholas Parish (RC)**)

Margaret Tighe (daughter):

Residence - 1 Nerney's Court - April 26, 1861

Michael Noonan, son of John Noonan & Elizabeth Unknown (son-in-law):

Residence - Sandymount - April 26, 1861

40 Cuffe Street - November 8, 1861

Wedding Witnesses:

Thomas Tighe & Elizabeth Tighe

Tighe Surname Ireland: 1600s to 1900s

o Elizabeth Tighe & Gulielmo Kennan – 25 Nov 1861 (Marriage, **St. Nicholas Parish (RC)**) & 10 Feb 1862 (Marriage, **St. Mary, Pro Cathedral Parish (RC)**)

Elizabeth Tighe (daughter):

Residence - 40 Cuffe Street - November 25, 1861

5 Nerney's Court - February 10, 1862

Gulielmo Kennan, son of Samuel Kennan & Catherine Unknown (son-in-law):

Residence - 40 Cuffe Street - November 25, 1861

8 Brunswick Place - February 10, 1862

Wedding Witnesses:

Michael Noonan & Anne Dunne

James Lynch & Sarah Tighe

o Sarah Tighe & Patrick Bowden – 16 Aug 1862 (Marriage, **St. Mary, Pro Cathedral Parish (RC)**)

■ Anne Bowden – b. 16 Jun 1863, bapt. 1 Jul 1863 (Baptism, **St. Mary, Pro Cathedral Parish (RC)**)

Sarah Tighe (daughter):

Residence - 6 Nerney's Court - August 16, 1862

Patrick Bowden, son of Richard Bowden & Bridget Unknown (son-in-law):

Residence - 6 Nerney's Court - August 16, 1862

July 1, 1863

Hurst

Wedding Witnesses:

Thomas Tighe & Mary Ryan

- John Tighe & Elizabeth Unknown
  - ○ Patrick Tighe & Mary Connell – 6 May 1867 (Marriage, **St. Michan Parish** (RC))

Patrick Tighe (son):

Residence - 18 Hay Market - May 6, 1867

Mary Connell, daughter of James Connell & Ellen Unknown (daughter-in-law):

Residence - Ormond Market - May 6, 1867

Wedding Witnesses:

Francis Crosbie & Catherine Connell

- John Tighe & Elizabeth Welds – 3 Feb 1839 (Marriage, **St. Andrew Parish** (RC))
  - ○ Thomas Tighe – bapt. 1839 (Baptism, **St. Andrew Parish** (RC))
  - ○ Bridget Tighe – bapt. 1846 (Baptism, **St. Andrew Parish** (RC))
- John Tighe & Grace Unknown
  - ○ Gulielmo Tighe – bapt. 31 Nov 1767 (Baptism, **St. Nicholas Parish** (RC))
  - ○ Mary Tighe – bapt. 3 Dec 1777 (Baptism, **St. Michan Parish** (RC))
  - ○ Peter Tighe – bapt. 20 Jun 1780 (Baptism, **St. Michan Parish** (RC))
  - ○ Michael Tighe – bapt. 13 Oct 1781 (Baptism, **St. Michan Parish** (RC))
- John Tighe & Jane Cahill – 29 Nov 1845 (Marriage, **St. James Parish** (RC))
  - ○ John Tighe – bapt. 10 Sep 1846 (Baptism, **St. James Parish** (RC))
  - ○ Mary Tighe – bapt. 29 Nov 1847 (Baptism, **St. James Parish** (RC))
  - ○ Thomas Tighe – bapt. 8 Nov 1849 (Baptism, **St. James Parish** (RC))

Tighe Surname Ireland: 1600s to 1900s

- ○ Jane Tighe – bapt. 3 Jul 1851 (Baptism, **St. James Parish** (RC))

- ○ Mary Josephine Tighe – bapt. 8 May 1854 (Baptism, **St. James Parish** (RC))

- ○ Susan Tighe – bapt. 14 Jul 1856 (Baptism, **St. James Parish** (RC))

- ○ Anne Tighe – b. 10 Feb 1859, bapt. 21 Feb 1859 (Baptism, **St. James Parish** (RC))

- ○ John Tighe – b. 8 Sep 1861, bapt. 23 Sep 1861 (Baptism, **St. James Parish** (RC))

John Tighe (father):

Residence - Dolphin's Barn - May 8, 1854

July 14, 1856

February 21, 1859

Grand Canal Baran Bridge - September 23, 1861

- • John Tighe & Jean Hurly

  - ○ James Tighe – bapt. 1 Apr 1838 (Baptism, **Drimoleague Parish** (RC))

- • John Tighe & Joan Kelly

  - ○ Ellen Tighe – bapt. 27 Jun 1831 (Baptism, **St. Mary, Pro Cathedral Parish** (RC))

  - ○ Mary Tighe – bapt. 13 Apr 1835 (Baptism, **St. Michan Parish** (RC))

  - ○ Mary Tighe – bapt. 30 Apr 1838 (Baptism, **St. Mary, Pro Cathedral Parish** (RC))

- • John Tighe & Margaret Fox

  - ○ Elizabeth Tighe – b. 1858, bapt. 15 Oct 1861 (Baptism, **St. Catherine Parish** (RC))

John Tighe (father):

Residence - Roscommon - October 15, 1861

Hurst

- John Tighe & Margaret Hetherson

  - Mary Tighe & Thomas Keating – 15 Nov 1863 (Marriage, **St. Michan Parish** (RC))

    - Patrick Keating – b. 21 Oct 1882, bapt. 3 Nov 1882 (Baptism, **St. Audoen Parish** (RC))

    - Anne Keating – b. 9 Sep 1885, bapt. 22 Sep 1885 (Baptism, **St. Audoen Parish** (RC))

    - Christopher John Keating – b. 22 Dec 1889, bapt. 31 Dec 1889 (Baptism, **St. Audoen Parish** (RC)

Mary Tighe (daughter):

Residence - 18 Anne Street - November 15, 1863

Thomas Keating, son of John Keating & Mary Unknown (son-in-law):

Residence - 18 Anne Street - November 15, 1863

12 Nicholas Street - November 3, 1882

September 22, 1885

December 31, 1889

  - Teresa Tighe – b. 21 Feb 1861, bapt. 1 Mar 1861 (Baptism, **St. Michan Parish** (RC))

  - John Tighe – b. 24 Sep 1863, bapt. 5 Oct 1863 (Baptism, **St. Michan Parish** (RC))

  - Charlotte Tighe – b. 22 Mar 1867, bapt. 22 Mar 1867 (Baptism, **St. Michan Parish** (RC))

John Tighe (father):

Residence - 25 Beresford Place - March 1, 1861

18 Anne Street - October 5, 1863

10 Anne Street - March 22, 1867

Tighe Surname Ireland: 1600s to 1900s

- John Tighe & Margaret Tighe

  - Mary Tighe & Timothy Flynn – 29 Aug 1865 (Marriage, **St. Mary, Pro Cathedral Parish (RC)**)

    - Catherine Sarah Flynn – b. 16 Mar 1866, bapt. 26 Mar 1866 (Baptism, **St. Michan Parish (RC)**)

Mary Tighe (daughter):

    Residence - Celbridge - August 29, 1865

Timothy Flynn, son of Timothy Flynn & Catherine Unknown (son-in-law):

    Residence - 24 Great Britain Street - August 29, 1865

        142 Upper Dorset Street - March 26, 1866

  - Patrick Tighe & Rose Anne Healey – 12 Feb 1871 (Marriage, **Chapelizod Parish (RC)**)

Patrick Tighe (son):

    Residence - Celbridge - February 12, 1871

Rose Anne Healey, daughter of Patrick Healey & Anne Cullen (daughter-in-law):

    Residence - Chapelizod - February 12, 1871

- John Tighe & Margaret Unknown

  - Michael Tighe & Anne Jane Reeves – 12 Aug 1877 (Marriage, **St. Nicholas Parish (RC)**)

    - Gulielmo Tighe – b. 4 Oct 1877, bapt. 5 Oct 1877 (Baptism, **St. Audoen Parish (RC)**)

    - Michael Tighe – b. 30 Mar 1880, bapt. 2 Apr 1880 (Baptism, **St. Audoen Parish (RC)**)

    - Robert Tighe, b. 24 May 1882, bapt. 26 May 1882 (Baptism, **St. Audoen Parish (RC)**) & Margaret Thorogood – 14 Feb 1904 (Marriage, **Harrington Street Parish (RC)**)

Hurst

Robert Tighe (son):

    Residence - 10 Richmond Place - February 14, 1904

Margaret Thorogood, daughter of John Thorogood & Anne Roberts

(daughter-in-law):

    Residence - 3 Pheasant's Place - February 14, 1904

- Joseph Tighe – b. 16 Oct 1884, bapt. 21 Oct 1884 (Baptism, St. Audoen Parish (RC))

- John Tighe – b. 21 Aug 1887, bapt. 23 Aug 1887 (Baptism, St. Audoen Parish (RC))

- Catherine Tighe – b. 6 Jan 1892, bapt. 12 Jan 1892 (Baptism, Harrington Street Parish (RC))

- Anne Jane Tighe – b. 27 Nov 1895, bapt. 3 Dec 1895 (Baptism, Harrington Street Parish (RC))

- Mary Teresa Tighe – b. 9 Aug 1899, bapt. 11 Aug 1899 (Baptism, Harrington Street Parish (RC))

Michael Tighe (son):

    Residence - 8 Corn Market - August 12, 1877

        12 Nicholas Street - October 5, 1877

            April 2, 1880

        10 Nicholas Street - May 26, 1882

            October 21, 1884

            August 23, 1887

        10 Richmond Street - January 12, 1892

Tighe Surname Ireland: 1600s to 1900s

10 South Richmond Place - December 3, 1895

10 Richmond Place - August 11, 1899

Anne Jane Reeves, daughter of John Reeves & Mary Unknown (daughter-in-law):

Residence - 7 Patrick Street - August 12, 1877

Wedding Witnesses:

Anthony Reeves & Margaret Tighe

- o Margaret Tighe & Anthony Reeves – 8 Jun 1879 (Marriage, **St. Audoen Parish (RC)**)
  - ▪ Anne Jane Reeves – b. 1880, bapt. 1880 (Baptism, **St. Andrew Parish (RC)**)

Margaret Tighe (daughter):

Residence - 8 Corn Market - June 8, 1879

Anthony Reeves, son of John Reeves (son-in-law):

Residence - 12 Nicholas Street - June 8, 1879

9 Luke Street - 1880

- John Tighe & Mary Hegarty
  - o Patrick Tighe – bapt. 15 Mar 1844 (Baptism, **Drimoleague Parish (RC)**)
- John Tighe & Mary Hurly
  - o Mary Tighe – bapt. 30 Oct 1842 (Baptism, **Drimoleague Parish (RC)**)
- John Tighe & Mary Jennet
  - o John Tighe – b. 17 Oct 1855, bapt. 2 Nov 1855 (Baptism, **St. Agatha Parish (RC)**)

John Tighe (father):

Residence - 9 Taaffes Place - November 2, 1855

Hurst

- John Tighe & Mary Keogh

  - Bridget Tighe – bapt. 12 Mar 1803 (Baptism, **St. Catherine Parish** (RC))

  - Frances Tighe – bapt. Aug 1807 (Baptism, **St. Nicholas Parish** (RC))

  - Anne Tighe – bapt. Mar 1815 (Baptism, **St. Nicholas Parish** (RC))

- John Tighe & Mary Kernan (K e r n a n)

  - Richard Tighe – bapt. 9 Apr 1803 (Baptism, **St. Michan Parish** (RC))

- John Tighe & Mary Kevelin

  - John Tighe – bapt. 27 Jul 1816 (Baptism, **St. Michan Parish** (RC))

- John Tighe & Mary Moriarty

  - Michael Tighe – b. 6 Nov 1805, bapt. 6 Nov 1805 (Baptism, **Tralee Parish** (RC))

  - Elizabeth Tighe – b. 24 Jan 1808, bapt. 24 Jan 1808 (Baptism, **Tralee Parish** (RC))

  - Mary Tighe – b. 22 Apr 1815, bapt. 22 Apr 1815 (Baptism, **Tralee Parish** (RC))

John Tighe (father):

Residence - Tralee - November 6, 1805

January 24, 1808

April 22, 1815

- John Tighe & Mary Oakman – 26 Jun 1805 (Marriage, **St. Mary, Pro Cathedral Parish** (RC))

  - Lucy Tighe – bapt. 17 Dec 1808 (Baptism, **St. Nicholas Parish** (RC))

  - Anne Tighe – bapt. 18 Mar 1810 (Baptism, **St. Nicholas Parish** (RC))

- John Tighe & Mary Regan

  - Michael Tighe – bapt. 6 Jan 1844 (Baptism, **Drimoleague Parish** (RC))

Tighe Surname Ireland: 1600s to 1900s

- John Tighe & Mary Tighe

  o John Tighe – bapt. 29 Aug 1830 (Baptism, **St. Mary, Pro Cathedral Parish** (RC))

- John Tighe & Mary Unknown

  o Thomas Tighe – bapt. 1820 (Baptism, **St. Andrew Parish** (RC))

- John Tighe & Mary Unknown

  o Christopher Tighe – bapt. 23 Mar 1849 (Baptism, **St. Catherine Parish** (RC))

- John Tighe & Mary Anne Brennan – 21 Sep 1847 (Marriage, **St. Catherine Parish** (RC))

- John Tighe & Mary Anne Howe

  o Jane Tighe & John Rogers – 19 Aug 1877 (Marriage, **St. Michan Parish** (RC))

    ▪ Christopher Joseph Rogers – b. 18 May 1878, bapt. 22 May 1878 (Baptism, **St. Michan Parish** (RC))

    ▪ Mary Catherine Rogers – b. 16 Jan 1880, bapt. 21 Jan 1880 (Baptism, **St. Michan Parish** (RC))

    ▪ John Patrick Rogers – b. 1881, bapt. 1881 (Baptism, **St. Andrew Parish** (RC))

    ▪ Jane Frances Rogers – b. 26 Jul 1883, bapt. 30 Jul 1883 (Baptism, **St. Mary, Pro Cathedral Parish** (RC))

    ▪ Christine Anne Rogers – b. 5 Dec 1886, bapt. 6 Dec 1886 (Baptism, **St. Mary, Pro Cathedral Parish** (RC))

    ▪ Charles Stewart Rogers – b. 6 Feb 1889, bapt. 8 Feb 1889 (Baptism, **St. Mary, Pro Cathedral Parish** (RC))

    ▪ Mary Anne Rogers – b. 7 Aug 1891, bapt. 10 Aug 1891 (Baptism, **St. Mary, Pro Cathedral Parish** (RC))

Hurst

Jane Tighe (daughter):

Residence - 67 Wellington Street - August 19, 1877

John Rogers, son of John Rogers & Catherine Unknown (son-in-law):

Residence - 94 Lower Mecklenburgh Street - August 19, 1877

68 Wellington Street - May 22, 1878

67 Lower Wellington Street - January 21, 1880

14 Cumberland Street - 1881

97 Capel Street - July 30, 1883

17 Findlater Place - December 6, 1886

August 10, 1891

3 Lower Gloucester Street - February 8, 1889

- o Mary Anne Tighe – b. 6 Sep 1866, bapt. 7 Sep 1866 (Baptism, **St. Michan Parish (RC)**)

- o Joseph Tighe – b. 29 Jul 1868, bapt. 29 Jul 1868 (Baptism, **St. Michan Parish (RC)**)

- o Cornelius (C o r n e l i u s) Tighe – b. 4 Sep 1869, bapt. 15 Sep 1869 (Baptism, **St. Michan Parish (RC)**)

- o Christopher Joseph Tighe – b. 29 Nov 1871, bapt. 1 Dec 1871 (Baptism, **St. Mary, Pro Cathedral Parish (RC)**)

John Tighe (father):

Residence - 68 Wellington Street - September 7, 1866

July 29, 1868

September 15, 1869

48

33 Cabe Lane - December 1, 1871

- John Tighe & Mary Anne Unknown

  - Francis Stephen Tighe – b. 2 Aug 1864, bapt. 3 Aug 1864 (Baptism, **St. Michan Parish (RC)**)

John Tighe (father):

Residence - 5 North Lisburn Street - August 3, 1864

- John Tighe & Sarah McCormick (M c C o r m i c k) – 13 Jun 1813 (Marriage, **St. Catherine Parish (RC)**)

  - Mary Tighe – bapt. 13 Jul 1814 (Baptism, **St. Catherine Parish (RC)**)

  - Patrick Tighe – b. 10 May 1816, bapt. 13 May 1816 (Baptism, **St. Catherine Parish (RC)**)

  - Catherine Tighe – bapt. 17 Jul 1825 (Baptism, **St. Nicholas Parish (RC)**)

  - Bridget Tighe – bapt. 28 Feb 1830 (Baptism, **St. Nicholas Parish (RC)**)

- John Tighe & Unknown

  - Mary Teresa Jane Tighe & Richard Blong – 20 Aug 1861 (Marriage, **St. Paul Parish**)

Signatures:

Mary Teresa Jane Tighe (daughter):

Residence - 6 Haymarket - August 20, 1861

Relationship Status at Marriage - minor age

Hurst

Richard Blong, son of Richard Blong (son-in-law):

    Residence - 5 Lower Bridge Street - August 20, 1861

    Occupation - Cattle Dealer - August 20, 1861

Richard Blong (father):

    Occupation - Cattle Dealer

John Tighe (father):

    Occupation - Cattle Dealer

Wedding Witnesses:

Richard Roberts & Thomas Browning

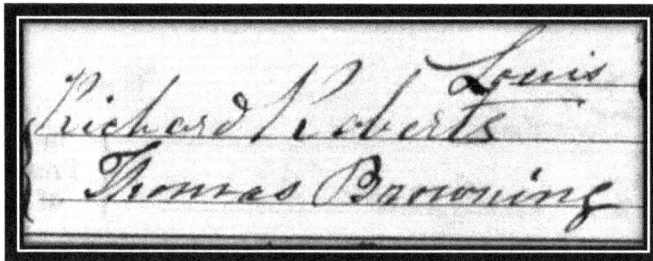

Signatures:

- John Tighe & Unknown
  - Mary Crumlin Tighe & Patrick Ennis – 29 Jun 1869 (Marriage, **St. James Parish (RC)**)
    - Mary Margaret Ennis – b. 1870, bapt. 1870 (Baptism, **St. Andrew Parish (RC)**)
    - John Patrick Ennis – b. 25 Feb 1876, bapt. 6 Mar 1876 (Baptism, **SS. Michael & John Parish (RC)**)

Mary Crumlin Tighe (daughter):

    Residence - Dolphin's Barn, Crumlin Road - June 29, 1869

Tighe Surname Ireland: 1600s to 1900s

Patrick Ennis, son of George Ennis (son-in-law):

Residence - 16 Peter's Row - June 29, 1869

27 South Stephen Street - 1870

28 Temple Bar - March 6, 1876

- John Tighe & Unknown
  - ○ Anne Mary Tighe – b. 28 Aug 1871, bapt. 7 Sep 1871 (Baptism, **St. Agatha Parish** (RC))

John Tighe (father):

Residence - 30 [Hard to Read] **Street** - September 7, 1871

- John Tighe & Unknown
  - ○ Jane Tighe & Patrick Doran – 26 Sep 1875 (Marriage, **St. James Parish** (RC))
    - ▪ Patrick Joseph Doran – b. 11 Jan 1885, bapt. 18 Jan 1885 (Baptism, **St. Joseph Parish** (RC))

Jane Tighe (daughter):

Residence - 8 Crumlin Road - September 26, 1875

Patrick Doran, son of Patrick Doran (son-in-law):

Residence - 69 Cork Street - September 26, 1875

Terenure - January 18, 1885

Wedding Witnesses:

Luke Doyle & Mary Tighe

Hurst

- John Tighe & Unknown

  - Francis Tighe & Elizabeth Byrne (B y r n e) – 11 Jun 1888 (Marriage, **St. Andrew Parish (RC)**)

Francis Tighe (son):

Residence - 17 Findlater Place - June 11, 1888

Elizabeth Byrne, daughter of Charles Byrne (daughter-in-law):

Residence - 116 Stephen's Place - June 11, 1888

- John Francis Tighe & Mary Barrington

  - John Patrick Tighe – b. 17 Aug 1877, bapt. 27 Aug 1877 (Baptism, **St. Michan Parish (RC)**)

  - Agnes Tighe – b. 20 Jan 1879, bapt. 29 Jan 1879 (Baptism, **St. Michan Parish (RC)**)

  - Margaret Mary Tighe – b. 12 Aug 1883, bapt. 17 Aug 1883 (Baptism, **St. Mary, Pro Cathedral Parish (RC)**)

  - James Joseph Tighe – b. 29 Mar 1886, bapt. 31 Mar 1886 (Baptism, **St. Mary, Pro Cathedral Parish (RC)**)

John Francis Tighe (father):

Residence - 33 Church Street - August 27, 1877

32 Church Street - January 29, 1879

27 Denmark Street - August 17, 1883

March 31, 1886

Tighe Surname Ireland: 1600s to 1900s

- John Malachi Tighe & Honor Teresa Burke

  - Hubert Malachi Tighe – b. 10 Apr 1863, bapt. .1 May 1863 (Baptism, **St. Lawrence Parish (RC)**)

  - Michael John Tighe – b. 9 Jun 1864, bapt. 24 Jun 1864 (Baptism, **St. Mary, Pro Cathedral Parish** (RC))

  - Patrick Francis Tighe – b. 2 Aug 1866, bapt. 10 Aug 1866 (Baptism, **St. Agatha Parish** (RC))

  - Joseph Tighe – b. 9 Jan 1871, bapt. 22 Jan 1871 (Baptism, **Rathmines Parish** (RC))

  - Mary Tighe – b. 8 Dec 1872, bapt. 18 Dec 1872 (Baptism, **St. Agatha Parish** (RC))

  - Mary Catherine Christine Josephine Tighe – b. 30 Apr 1874, bapt. 11 May 1874 (Baptism, **St. Agatha Parish** (RC))

  - Brendan Tighe – b. 10 Sep 1875, bapt. 11 Sep 1875 (Baptism, **St. Audoen Parish** (RC))

  - Honor Mary Clare Tighe – b. 8 Aug 1876, bapt. 15 Aug 1876 (Baptism, **St. Audoen Parish** (RC))

  - McCartin Hubert Mary Tighe – b. 24 May 1878, bapt. 31 May 1878 (Baptism, **St. Audoen Parish** (RC))

  - Aloysius Tighe – b. 14 Jun 1880, bapt. 21 Jun 1880 (Baptism, **St. Andrew Parish** (RC))

  - Gertrude Agnes Mary Tighe – b. 24 Feb 1888, bapt. 28 Feb 1888 (Baptism, **St. Agatha Parish** (RC))

John Malachi Tighe (father):

Residence - Annesley Cottage, North Strand - May 1, 1863

143 Lower Gloucester Street - June 24, 1864

21 Portland Street - August 10, 1866

Hurst

Harrington Terrace - January 22, 1871

3 North Richmond Street - December 18, 1872

May 11, 1874

20 Lower Bridge Street - September 11, 1875

August 15, 1876

May 31, 1878

6 Foyle Terrace - June 21, 1880

2 Richmond Street - February 28, 1888

- Joseph Tighe & Bridget Unknown
  - Michael Tighe – bapt. 7 Feb 1847 (Baptism, St. Mary, Pro Cathedral Parish (RC))
- Joseph Tighe & Catherine Hennessey
  - Joseph Tighe – b. 4 Jun 1861, bapt. 7 Jun 1861 (Baptism, St. Nicholas Parish (RC))

Joseph Tighe (father):

Residence - 24 Golden Lane - June 7, 1861

- Joseph Tighe & Catherine Spellacy – 31 Jan 1853 (Marriage, St. Nicholas Parish (RC))
  - John Tighe – b. 13 Jan 1854, bapt. 25 Jan 1854 (Baptism, St. Nicholas Parish (RC))
  - Mary Tighe – b. 6 Apr 1856, bapt. 16 Apr 1856 (Baptism, St. Nicholas Parish (RC))
  - William Tighe – b. 11 Feb 1858, bapt. 26 Feb 1858 (Baptism, St. Nicholas Parish (RC))
  - Joseph Tighe – b. 14 Oct 1870, bapt. 24 Oct 1870 (Baptism, St. Nicholas Parish (RC))
  - Catherine Tighe – b. 2 Mar 1872, bapt. 18 Mar 1873 (Baptism, St. Nicholas Parish (RC))
  - James Tighe – b. 29 Jul 1873, bapt. 8 Aug 1873 (Baptism, St. Nicholas Parish (RC))

Tighe Surname Ireland: 1600s to 1900s

Joseph Tighe (father):

Residence - 24 Golden Lane - January 25, 1854

February 26, 1858

October 24, 1870

14 Bride's Street - April 16, 1856

38 Golden Lane - March 18, 1872

38 Golden Street - August 8, 1873

- Joseph Tighe & Unknown

  o Mary Tighe & Joseph Dalton – 7 Aug 1876 (Marriage, **St. Audoen Parish (RC)**)

    ▪ Mary Jane Dalton – b. 17 May 1877, bapt. 28 May 1877 (Baptism, **SS. Michael & John Parish (RC)**)

    ▪ James Dalton – b. 2 Dec 1878, bapt. 12 Dec 1878 (Baptism, **SS. Michael & John Parish (RC)**)

    ▪ Agnes Dalton – b. 22 Jan 1885, bapt. 26 Jan 1885 (Baptism, **SS. Michael & John Parish (RC)**)

    ▪ John Dalton – b. 30 Aug 1887, bapt. 5 Sep 1887 (Baptism, **SS. Michael & John Parish (RC)**)

Mary Tighe (daughter):

Residence - 8 Werburgh Street - August 7, 1876

Joseph Dalton, son of James Dalton (son-in-law):

Residence - 48 Fishamble Street - August 7, 1876

Hurst

31 Castle Street - May 28, 1877

9 Upper Exchequer Street - December 12, 1878

13 Wood Quay - January 26, 1885

27 Mercer Street - September 5, 1887

- Joshua Tighe & Bridget Unknown
  - William Tighe – bapt. 20 Jul 1845 (Baptism, *St. Mary, Pro Cathedral Parish* (RC))
- Joshua Tighe & Catherine Unknown
  - Anne Tighe – bapt. 7 Mar 1820 (Baptism, *St. Mary, Pro Cathedral Parish* (RC))

Joshua Tighe (father):

Residence - Church Street, L H - March 7, 1820

- Joshua Tighe & Mary Unknown
  - Joshua Tighe – bapt. 12 Nov 1822 (Baptism, *St. Mary, Pro Cathedral Parish* (RC))

Joshua Tighe (father):

Residence - Moor Lane - November 12, 1822

- L. Tighe & Catherine Reilly
  - Sarah Tighe – bapt. 10 Jun 1815 (Baptism, *SS. Michael & John Parish* (RC))
- Lawrence Tighe & Bridget Murphy
  - Francis Tighe – bapt. 23 Dec 1781 (Baptism, *St. Catherine Parish* (RC))
- Lawrence Tighe & Bridget Unknown
  - John Tighe – b. 1767, bapt. 25 Jul 1767 (Baptism, *St. Catherine Parish* (RC))

Tighe Surname Ireland: 1600s to 1900s

- Lawrence Tighe & Christine Unknown

  - James Tighe – bapt. 1778 (Baptism, **St. Andrew Parish** (RC))

  - Michael Tighe – bapt. 1779 (Baptism, **St. Andrew Parish** (RC))

  - Thomas Tighe – bapt. 1782 (Baptism, **St. Andrew Parish** (RC))

  - Eleanor Tighe – bapt. 1785 (Baptism, **St. Andrew Parish** (RC))

- Lawrence Tighe & Elizabeth Unknown

  - George Tighe – bapt. 1767 (Baptism, **St. Andrew Parish** (RC))

  - Peter Tighe – bapt. 1771 (Baptism, **St. Andrew Parish** (RC))

- Lawrence Tighe & Ellen Minihane – 2 Sep 1835 (Marriage, **Rossalettiri & Kilkeraunmor (Roscarbery & Lissevard) Parish** (RC))

- Lawrence Tighe & Mary Field

  - James Tighe – bapt. 7 Jan 1786 (Baptism, **St. Catherine Parish** (RC))

  - Lawrence Tighe – bapt. 12 Dec 1786 (Baptism, **St. Catherine Parish** (RC))

  - Mary Tighe – bapt. 15 May 1789 (Baptism, **St. Catherine Parish** (RC))

  - Charlotte Tighe – bapt. 9 Aug 1790 (Baptism, **St. Catherine Parish** (RC))

- Lawrence Tighe & Mary Unknown

  - Mary Tighe – bapt. 11 Aug 1755 (Baptism, **St. Michan Parish** (RC))

  - Eleanor Tighe – bapt. 7 Nov 1757 (Baptism, **St. Michan Parish** (RC))

  - Lawrence Tighe – bapt. 29 Jan 1760 (Baptism, **St. Michan Parish** (RC))

- Lawrence Tighe & Mary Unknown

  - Lawrence Tighe – bapt. 1761 (Baptism, **St. Andrew Parish** (RC))

- Leonard Tighe & Catherine Unknown

  - Michael Tighe – bapt. 12 Jan 1806 (Baptism, **St. Mary, Pro Cathedral Parish** (RC))

Hurst

- Leonard Tighe & Catherine Unknown

  - Edward O'Reilly Tighe – bapt. 1812 (Baptism, **Clondalkin Parish (RC)**)

- Lewis Tighe & Catherine Unknown

  - Mary Tighe – bapt. 21 Dec 1806 (Baptism, **St. Mary, Pro Cathedral Parish (RC)**)

- Malachi Tighe & Elizabeth Unknown

  - Patrick Tighe – bapt. 10 Dec 1838 (Baptism, **St. Mary, Pro Cathedral Parish (RC)**)

  - Elizabeth Tighe – bapt. 14 Mar 1841 (Baptism, **St. Mary, Pro Cathedral Parish (RC)**)

  - Harriet Tighe – bapt. 16 Nov 1845 (Baptism, **St. Mary, Pro Cathedral Parish (RC)**)

- Mark Tighe & Mary Unknown

  - Thomas Tighe – bapt. 1802 (Baptism, **St. Andrew Parish (RC)**)

  - John Tighe – bapt. 1805 (Baptism, **St. Andrew Parish (RC)**)

  - Unknown Tighe – bapt. 1808 (Baptism, **St. Andrew Parish (RC)**)

  - Esther Tighe – bapt. 1811 (Baptism, **St. Andrew Parish (RC)**)

  - Mary Tighe – bapt. 1814 (Baptism, **St. Andrew Parish (RC)**)

  - John Tighe – bapt. 1819 (Baptism, **St. Andrew Parish (RC)**)

- Martin Tighe & Esther Edwards – 6 Jan 1834 (Marriage, **St. Catherine Parish (RC)**)

  - Jane Tighe – bapt. 10 May 1835 (Baptism, **St. James Parish (RC)**)

  - Sarah Tighe – bapt. 27 Feb 1837 (Baptism, **St. James Parish (RC)**)

  - John Tighe – bapt. 3 Jun 1839 (Baptism, **St. James Parish (RC)**)

  - James Tighe, bapt. 16 Aug 1841 (Baptism, **St. James Parish (RC)**) & Mary Carmichael

    (C a r m i c h a e l) – 12 Jan 1868 (Marriage, **St. Mary, Pro Cathedral Parish (RC)**)

James Tighe (son):

Residence - 89 Britain Street - January 12, 1868

Tighe Surname Ireland: 1600s to 1900s

Mary Carmichael, daughter of John Carmichael & Anne Unknown

(daughter-in-law):

Residence - 210 Britain Street - January 12, 1868

- o Anne Tighe – bapt. 28 Dec 1844 (Baptism, **St. Catherine Parish** (RC))

- o William Tighe – bapt. 13 Mar 1848 (Baptism, **St. James Parish** (RC))

Wedding Witnesses:

John Edwards & Bridget Gibney

- Martin Tighe & Mary Caffrey

  - o Martin Tighe – b. 12 Apr 1858, bapt. 22 Apr 1858 (Baptism, **St. James Parish** (RC))

Martin Tighe (father):

Residence - Inchicore - April 22, 1858

- Martin Tighe & Mary Gaffney

  - o Martin Tighe – bapt. 12 Jun 1850 (Baptism, **St. Nicholas Parish** (RC))

- Martin Tighe & Mary Unknown

  - o Thomas Tighe & Margaret Loughlin – 15 May 1870 (Marriage, **St. Nicholas Parish** (RC))

Thomas Tighe (son):

Residence - 10 Patrick Street - May 15, 1870

Margaret Loughlin, daughter of Cornelius Loughlin & Jane Unknown

(daughter-in-law):

Residence - 10 Patrick Street - May 15, 1870

Hurst

- Martin Tighe & Unknown
  - Catherine Tighe & Patrick Ennis – 12 Feb 1882 (Marriage, **St. Audoen Parish (RC)**)

Catherine Tighe (daughter):

Residence - 12 Back Lane - February 12, 1882

Patrick Ennis, son of John Ennis (son-in-law):

Residence - 12 Back Lane - February 12, 1882

- Matthew Tighe & Anne Unknown
  - Mary Tighe – bapt. 6 Oct 1747 (Baptism, **St. Michan Parish (RC)**)
  - Anne Tighe – bapt. 30 May 1749 (Baptism, **St. Michan Parish (RC)**)
- Matthew Tighe & Bridget Unknown
  - Catherine Tighe & Martin Brennan – 6 Nov 1870 (Marriage, **St. Andrew Parish (RC)**)

Catherine Tighe (daughter):

Residence - 15 Deuzille Street - November 6, 1870

Martin Brennan, son of William Brennan & Anne Unknown (son-in-law):

Residence - 15 Deuzille Street - November 6, 1870

- Matthew Tighe & Catherine Unknown
  - Patrick Tighe – bapt. 5 Dec 1742 (Baptism, **St. Michan Parish (RC)**)

Matthew Tighe (father):

Residence - Mary's Lane - December 5, 1742

Tighe Surname Ireland: 1600s to 1900s

- Matthew Tighe & Elizabeth Tucker

  o Thomas Arthur Tighe – bapt. 13 May 1887 (Baptism, **SS. Michael & John Parish (RC)**)

Thomas Arthur Tighe (son):

Remarks about Birth - died

- Matthew Tighe & Elizabeth Whitten

  o Mary Tighe – b. 27 Jan 1874, bapt. 9 Mar 1874 (Baptism, **St. Joseph Parish (RC)**)

Matthew Tighe (father):

Residence - Lodge of Laurel Lodge, Kimmage Road - March 9, 1874

- Matthew Tighe & Judith Curry – 9 May 1752 (Marriage, **St. Michan Parish (RC)**)

  o Margaret Tighe – bapt. 30 May 1753 (Baptism, **St. Michan Parish (RC)**)

  o Catherine Tighe – bapt. 20 Nov 1754 (Baptism, **St. Michan Parish (RC)**)

  o Mary Tighe – bapt. 1 Jul 1756 (Baptism, **St. Michan Parish (RC)**)

- Matthew Tighe & Margaret Callahan

  o Michael Tighe – bapt. 1817 (Baptism, **Clondalkin Parish (RC)**)

- Matthew Tighe & Mary Unknown

  o Anne Tighe – b. 1807, bapt. 27 Dec 1807 (Baptism, **St. Catherine Parish**)

Matthew Tighe (father):

Residence - Pimlico - December 27, 1807

- Matthew Tighe & Mary Unknown

  o James Tighe – bapt. 1822 (Baptism, **Clondalkin Parish (RC)**)

Hurst

- Matthew Tighe & Unknown

  o James A. Tighe & Mary Catherine Kelly – 8 Jan 1888 (Marriage, **St. James Parish** (RC))

James A. Tighe (son):

Residence - 7 Thomas Davis Street - January 8, 1888

Mary Catherine Kelly, daughter of John Kelly (daughter-in-law):

Residence - 7 Thomas David Street - January 8, 1888

- Matthew Francis Tighe & Mary Delahoyde

  o Peter Joseph Tighe – b. 1859, bapt. 1859 (Baptism, **Clondalkin Parish** (RC))

  o Francis Thomas Tighe – b. 1860, bapt. 1860 (Baptism, **Clondalkin Parish** (RC))

  o Matthew Tighe – b. 1863, bapt. 1863 (Baptism, **Clondalkin Parish** (RC))

  o Mary Josephine Tighe, b. 1865, bapt. 1865 (Baptism, **Clondalkin Parish** (RC)) & Simon

    Woods – 24 Apr 1884 (Marriage, **Clondalkin Parish** (RC))

Mary Tighe (daughter):

Residence - Clondalkin - April 24, 1884

Simon Woods, son of Andrew Woods & Anne Unknown (son-in-law):

Residence - Lower Clonborris - April 24, 1884

- o David Robert Tighe – b. 1867, bapt. 1867 (Baptism, **Clondalkin Parish** (RC))

  o William Joseph Tighe – b. 1869, bapt. 1869 (Baptism, **Clondalkin Parish** (RC))

  o Emily Margaret Tighe – b. 1871, bapt. 1871 (Baptism, **Clondalkin Parish** (RC))

  o Josephine Mary Tighe – b. 1873, bapt. 1873 (Baptism, **Clondalkin Parish** (RC))

  o Teresa Mary Tighe – b. 1875, bapt. 1875 (Baptism, **Clondalkin Parish** (RC))

Tighe Surname Ireland: 1600s to 1900s

Matthew Francis Tighe (father):

Residence - 9th Lock, Clondalkin - 1859

1860

1873

1875

Neilstown - 1863

1865

1867

1869

1871

- Michael Tighe & Alice Corcoran

  o Thomas Tighe – bapt. 4 Nov 1815 (Baptism, **St. Catherine Parish (RC)**)

- Michael Tighe & Anne Coleman – 1850 (Marriage, **St. Nicholas Parish (RC)**)

  o John Joseph Tighe – bapt. 25 Jun 1852 (Baptism, **St. Nicholas Parish (RC)**)

  o Elizabeth Tighe – b. 11 Apr 1854, bapt. 24 Apr 1854 (Baptism, **St. Nicholas Parish (RC)**)

  o Michael Thomas Tighe – b. 21 Oct 1856, bapt. 5 Nov 1856 (Baptism, **St. Nicholas Parish (RC)**)

Michael Tighe (father):

Residence - Britain Street Hospital, 22 Bride's Street - April 24, 1854

22 Bride's Street - November 5, 1856

Hurst

- Michael Tighe & Anne Finnigan

  o Christopher Tighe – b. 1 Jul 1854, bapt. 8 Jul 1854 (Baptism, **St. Mary, Pro Cathedral Parish** (RC))

Michael Tighe (father):

Residence - Santry Mother in Lower Hospital - July 8, 1854

- Michael Tighe & Bridget Nowlan – 23 Jun 1792 (Marriage, **St. Nicholas Parish** (RC))

Wedding Witnesses:

James Savage & John Nowlan

- Michael Tighe & Catherine Donovan

  o Mary Tighe – bapt. 5 Aug 1838 (Baptism, **Drimoleague Parish** (RC))

- Michael Tighe & Christian Maguire – 23 Jan 1758 (Marriage, **St. Michan Parish** (RC))

  o Nicholas Tighe – bapt. 17 May 1775 (Baptism, **St. Catherine Parish** (RC))

- Michael Tighe & Elizabeth Esterby

  o Hugh Tighe – bapt. 31 Aug 1834 (Baptism, **St. Nicholas Parish** (RC))

- Michael Tighe & Elizabeth Monks – 6 Jun 1834 (Marriage, **St. Audoen Parish** (RC))

  o James Tighe – bapt. 28 Jun 1837 (Baptism, **St. Audoen Parish** (RC))

  o Hugh Tighe – bapt. 27 Jul 1842 (Baptism, **St. Audoen Parish** (RC))

  o Michael Tighe – bapt. 28 Jun 1844 (Baptism, **St. Audoen Parish** (RC))

  o Christopher Tighe – bapt. 14 Jun 1847 (Baptism, **St. Audoen Parish** (RC))

- Michael Tighe & Elizabeth Tighe

  o Margaret Tighe – bapt. 18 Feb 1829 (Baptism, **St. Mary, Pro Cathedral Parish** (RC))

Tighe Surname Ireland: 1600s to 1900s

Michael Tighe (father):

Residence - Abbey Street - February 18, 1829

- Michael Tighe & Elizabeth Unknown

  o Michael Tighe – bapt. 5 Jun 1825 (Baptism, **St. Mary, Pro Cathedral Parish** (RC))

- Michael Tighe & Elizabeth Unknown

  o Patrick Tighe & Jane Christine Brennan – 20 Jul 1862 (Marriage, **St. Andrew Parish** (RC))

    ▪ Patrick Michael Tighe – b. 17 Aug 1865, bapt. 25 Aug 1865 (Baptism, **St. Nicholas Parish**

      (RC))

    ▪ James Joseph Tighe – b. 10 Jun 1868, bapt. 12 Jun 1868 (Baptism, **St. Nicholas Parish**

      (RC))

    ▪ Elizabeth Tighe – b. 1 Oct 1871, bapt. 2 Oct 1871 (Baptism, **St. Nicholas Parish** (RC))

    ▪ Sarah Tighe – b. 2 Oct 1871, bapt. 2 Oct 1871 (Baptism, **St. Nicholas Parish** (RC))

    ▪ Christine Julie Tighe – b. 17 Sep 1874, bapt. 18 Sep 1874 (Baptism, **St. Nicholas Parish**

      (RC))

Patrick Tighe (son):

Residence - 4 Peter's Row - July 20, 1862

Patrick Street - August 25, 1865

1 Little Ship Street - June 12, 1868

October 2, 1871

27 Little Ship Street - September 18, 1874

Hurst

Jane Christine Brennan, daughter of Patrick Brennan & Sarah Unknown

(daughter-in-law):

Residence - 161 Townsend Street - July 20, 1862

- Michael Tighe & Elizabeth Unknown
  - Christopher Tighe & Elizabeth Dunne – 20 Aug 1871 (Marriage, **St. Andrew Parish** (RC))
    - Michael John Tighe – b. 1872, bapt. 1872 (Baptism, **St. Andrew Parish** (RC))
    - Edward Christopher Tighe – b. 1874, bapt. 1874 (Baptism, **St. Andrew Parish** (RC))
    - Christopher Tighe – b. 1876, bapt. 1876 (Baptism, **St. Andrew Parish** (RC))
    - Elizabeth Mary Tighe – b. 1878, bapt. 1878 (Baptism, **St. Andrew Parish** (RC))
    - Mary Tighe – b. 1880, bapt. 1880 (Baptism, **St. Andrew Parish** (RC))
    - Teresa Tighe – b. 1883, bapt. 1883 (Baptism, **St. Andrew Parish** (RC))

Christopher Tighe (son):

Residence - 6 Fade Street - August 20, 1871

25 Cumberland Street - 1872

1874

20 Cumberland Street - 1878

1880

5 Grant's Row - 1883

Elizabeth Dunne, daughter of Edward Dunne & Elizabeth Unknown

(daughter-in-law):

Residence - 3 Merrion Row - August 20, 1871

Tighe Surname Ireland: 1600s to 1900s

- Michael Tighe & Elizabeth Wilson

  o Margaret Tighe – bapt. 2 Jun 1805 (Baptism, **St. James Parish** (RC))

- Michael Tighe & Ellen Draddy – 19 Jul 1877 (Marriage, **Cork - South Parish** (RC))

- Michael Tighe & Margaret Carberry

  o Margaret Frances Tighe – b. 2 Nov 1865, bapt. 8 Nov 1865 (Baptism, **St. Agatha Parish** (RC))

Michael Tighe (father):

Residence - 2 Nottingham Parade - November 8, 1865

- Michael Tighe & Margaret Unknown

  o Mary Tighe – bapt. Apr 1826 (Baptism, **St. James Parish** (RC))

- Michael Tighe & Margaret Mary Craddock

  o Margaret Tighe – bapt. 6 Jul 1774 (Baptism, **St. Catherine Parish** (RC))

  o Matthew Tighe – bapt. 1 Oct 1775 (Baptism, **St. Catherine Parish** (RC))

- Michael Tighe & Mary Carroll – 27 Jan 1823 (Marriage, **SS. Michael & John Parish** (RC))

  o Elizabeth Tighe – bapt. 4 Nov 1823 (Baptism, **St. James Parish** (RC))

  o Mary Tighe – bapt. 26 Jun 1825 (Baptism, **St. James Parish** (RC))

  o Michael Tighe – bapt. 20 Dec 1832 (Baptism, **St. James Parish** (RC))

  o John Tighe – bapt. 5 May 1834 (Baptism, **St. James Parish** (RC))

- Michael Tighe & Mary Shepherd – 18 Mar 1806 (Marriage, **St. Andrew Parish** (RC))

- Michael Tighe & Mary Tierney (T i e r n e y)

  o Michael Tighe – b. 1867, bapt. 1867 (Baptism, **St. Andrew Parish** (RC))

Hurst

Michael Tighe (father):

Residence - 25 Upper Mercer Street - 1867

- Michael Tighe & Mary Tighe

  o Patrick Tighe – bapt. 9 Nov 1835 (Baptism, **St. Mary, Pro Cathedral Parish (RC)**)

- Michael Tighe & Mary Unknown

  o Thomas Tighe – b. 1767, bapt. 27 Apr 1767 (Baptism, **St. Catherine Parish (RC)**)

- Michael Tighe & Roseanne Catherine Lawlor – 28 Sep 1856 (Marriage, **Rathfarnham Parish (RC)**)

  o Mary Tighe – b. 1857, bapt. 1857 (Baptism, **St. Andrew Parish (RC)**)

  o Michael Christopher Tighe – b. 18 Dec 1859, bapt. 26 Dec 1859 (Baptism, **St. Nicholas Parish (RC)**)

  o Roseanne Tighe – b. 11 May 1862, bapt. 19 May 1862 (Baptism, **St. Nicholas Parish (RC)**)

  o Michael Tighe – b. 9 Jun 1864, bapt. 13 Jun 1864 (Baptism, **St. Nicholas Parish (RC)**)

  o Michael Tighe – b. 15 Jul 1865, bapt. 31 Jul 1865 (Baptism, **St. Nicholas Parish (RC)**)

  o Michael John Tighe – b. 29 Sep 1867, bapt. 7 Oct 1867 (Baptism, **St. Nicholas Parish (RC)**)

  o Elizabeth Tighe – b. 21 Dec 1869, bapt. 3 Jan 1870 (Baptism, **St. Nicholas Parish (RC)**)

  o Catherine Tighe – b. 22 May 1872, bapt. 3 Jun 1872 (Baptism, **St. Nicholas Parish (RC)**)

  o Anne Jane Tighe – b. 6 Dec 1874, bapt. 14 Dec 1874 (Baptism, **St. Nicholas Parish (RC)**)

  o Myles Tighe – b. 17 May 1877, bapt. 28 May 1877 (Baptism, **St. Nicholas Parish (RC)**)

  o Thomas Christopher Tighe – b. 17 Dec 1878, bapt. 27 Dec 1878 (Baptism, **St. Nicholas Parish (RC)**)

Tighe Surname Ireland: 1600s to 1900s

Michael Tighe (father):

Residence - 3 Bishop Street - December 28, 1859

3 Bishop Court - May 19, 1862

June 13, 1864

July 31, 1865

October 7, 1867

January 3, 1870

December 14, 1874

May 28, 1877

December 27, 1878

7 Bishop Court - June 3, 1872

- Michael Tighe & Susan Webb
  - Susan Tighe – bapt. 28 Feb 1808 (Baptism, **St. Catherine Parish (RC)**)
  - Cecelia Tighe – bapt. 23 Jan 1810 (Baptism, **St. Catherine Parish (RC)**)
- Michael Tighe & Unknown
  - Thomas Tighe (1st Marriage) & Margaret Tighe
    - John Tighe – b. 15 Aug 1845, bapt. 31 Aug 1845 (Baptism, **St. Werburgh Parish**)
    - Susan Tighe, b. 9 Jul 1848, bapt. 30 Jul 1848 (Baptism, **St. Werburgh Parish**) & Patrick Edward Frederick Wheeler – 1 Oct 1893 (Marriage, **St. Werburgh Parish**)

Signatures:

Susan Tighe (daughter):

    Residence - 10 Castle Street - October 1, 1893

Patrick Edward Frederick Wheeler, son of Henry Wheeler (son-in-law):

    Residence - 13 North Portland Street - October 1, 1893

    Occupation - Book Keeper - October 1, 1893

Henry Wheeler (father):

    Occupation - Shoemaker

Thomas Tighe (father):

    Occupation - Tailor

Wedding Witnesses:

Maurice McGuinness & Hannah Tighe

Signatures:

Tighe Surname Ireland: 1600s to 1900s

- Margaret Tighe, b. 8 Sep 1851, bapt. 21 Sep 1851 (Baptism, **St. Werburgh Parish**) & John Joseph McGlynn – 3 Jan 1884 (Marriage, **St. Werburgh Parish**)

Signatures:

- Thomas Sidney McGlynn – b. 12 Feb 1885, bapt. 18 Feb 1885 (Baptism, **St. Mary, Pro Cathedral Parish (RC)**)

- Mary McGlynn – b. 5 Aug 1886, bapt. 9 Aug 1886 (Baptism, **SS. Michael & John Parish (RC)**)

- Susan McGlynn – b. 29 Apr 1890, bapt. 5 May 1890 (Baptism, **SS. Michael & John Parish (RC)**)

- John James McGlynn – b. 21 Jun 1892, bapt. 27 Jun 1892 (Baptism, **SS. Michael & John Parish (RC)**)

Margaret Tighe (daughter):

Residence - 8 Castle Street - January 3, 1884

John Joseph McGlynn, son of James McGlynn (son-in-law):

Residence - 8 Castle Street - January 3, 1884

May 5, 1890

19 Lower Dorset Street - February 18, 1885

11 Castle Street - August 9, 1886

Hurst

June 27, 1892

Occupation - Caustic Tiler - January 3, 1884

James McGlynn (father):

Occupation - Caustic Tiler

Thomas Tighe (father):

Occupation - Tailor

Wedding Witnesses:

Matthew Pinttard, M. McGuinness & Catherine O'Keefe

Signatures:

- Hannah Tighe – b. 3 Jul 1857, bapt. 26 Jul 1857 (Baptism, **St. Werburgh Parish**)

Signature:

- Nicholas Tighe – b. 1 Aug 1861, bapt. 25 Aug 1861 (Baptism, **St. Werburgh Parish**)
- Thomas Tighe (2nd Marriage) & Susan Flood – 8 Oct 1863 (Marriage, **St. Werburgh Parish**)

Tighe Surname Ireland: 1600s to 1900s

Signatures:

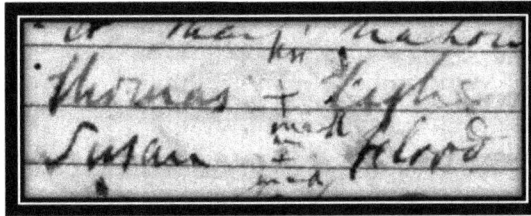

Thomas Tighe (son):

Residence - 1 Fishamble Street - August 31, 1845

 37 Castle Street - July 30, 1848

  September 21, 1851

 10 St. Werburgh Street - July 26, 1857

  August 25, 1861

  October 8, 1863

Occupation - Tailor - August 31, 1845

 July 30, 1848

 September 21, 1851

 July 26, 1857

 August 25, 1861

Hurst

October 8, 1863

Relationship Status at 2nd Marriage - widow

Susan Flood (2nd wife), daughter of George Flood (daughter-in-law):

Residence - 39 Castle Street - October 8, 1863

George Flood (father):

Occupation - Shoemaker

Michael Tighe (father):

Occupation - Tailor

Wedding Witnesses:

Lewis Flood & Mary Flint

Signatures:

- Murtagh Tighe & Elizabeth Jackson
  - Catherine Holmes – bapt. 7 Sep 1863 (Baptism, St. Mary, Pro Cathedral Parish (RC))

Tighe Surname Ireland: 1600s to 1900s

Murtagh Tighe (father):

   Residence - 2 Mecklenburgh Lane - September 7, 1863

- Nicholas Tighe & Mary Morrison

    o Julie Mary Tighe – bapt. 19 Aug 1836 (Baptism, **St. Nicholas Parish** (RC))

- Nicholas Tighe & Mary Unknown

    o Nicholas Tighe & Catherine Greene – 23 May 1862 (Marriage, **St. Michan Parish** (RC))

Nicholas Tighe (son):

   Residence - 11 North Frederick Street - May 23, 1862

Catherine Greene, daughter of Patrick Greene & Mary Anne Unknown

(daughter-in-law):

   Residence - Mountjoy Prison, North Circular Road - May 23, 1862

- Owen Tighe & Catherine Fox

    o Catherine Tighe – bapt. 13 Dec 1801 (Baptism, **Cork - South Parish** (RC))

Owen Tighe (father):

   Residence - Lodging - December 13, 1801

- Owen Tighe & Margaret Byrne (B y r n e)

    o Patrick Tighe – bapt. 1832 (Baptism, **St. Mary Parish** (RC))

    o Mary Tighe – bapt. 1834 (Baptism, **St. Mary Parish** (RC))

- Owen Tighe & Margaret Unknown

    o Mary Tighe – bapt. 9 Nov 1827 (Baptism, **St. Mary, Pro Cathedral Parish** (RC))

    o Catherine Tighe – bapt. 7 Oct 1830 (Baptism, **St. Mary, Pro Cathedral Parish** (RC))

Hurst

Owen Tighe (father):

Residence - Leeson Street - November 9, 1827

- Owen Tighe & Margaret Unknown
  - Julie Tighe – bapt. 1838 (Baptism, **St. Andrew Parish** (RC))
- Owen Tighe & Mary Stretch
  - Bridget Tighe & Thomas Walsh – 28 Nov 1867 (Marriage, **St. Lawrence Parish** (RC))
    - James Walsh – b. 27 Oct 1868, bapt. 30 Oct 1868 (Baptism, **St. Lawrence Parish** (RC))
    - Mary Eleanor Walsh – b. 15 Jun 1870, bapt. 17 Jun 1870 (Baptism, **St. Lawrence Parish** (RC))
    - Bridget Walsh – b. 9 Oct 1871, bapt. 11 Oct 1871 (Baptism, **St. Lawrence Parish** (RC))
    - Catherine Teresa Walsh – b. 10 Mar 1873, bapt. 12 Mar 1873 (Baptism, **St. Lawrence Parish** (RC))
    - Thomas Walsh – b. 19 Sep 1874, bapt. 22 Sep 1874 (Baptism, **St. Lawrence Parish** (RC))
    - Gulielmo Sheridan Walsh – b. 28 Apr 1876, bapt. 5 May 1876 (Baptism, **St. Lawrence Parish** (RC))

Bridget Tighe (daughter):

Residence - 36 Guild Street - November 28, 1867

Thomas Walsh, son of James Walsh & Martha Kirwan (son-in-law):

Residence - 53 North Wall - November 28, 1867

39 Guild Street - October 30, 1868

June 17, 1870

Tighe Surname Ireland: 1600s to 1900s

27 Guild Street - October 11, 1871

March 12, 1873

September 22, 1874

May 5, 1876

- o Ellen Tighe & James Flood – 24 Sep 1872 (Marriage, **St. Lawrence Parish** (RC))

  - Mary Anne Flood – b. 5 Nov 1873, bapt. 7 Nov 1873 (Baptism, **St. Lawrence Parish** (RC))

  - Patrick Flood – b. 15 Dec 1874, bapt. 18 Dec 1874 (Baptism, **St. Lawrence Parish** (RC))

  - Catherine Flood – b. 4 Feb 1876, bapt. 8 Feb 1876 (Baptism, **St. Lawrence Parish** (RC))

James Flood, son of Patrick Flood & Anne Armstrong (son-in-law):

Residence - Blythe's Avenue - November 7, 1873

37 Blythe's Avenue - December 18, 1874

37 Blythe's Avenue, Church Road - February 8, 1876

Wedding Witnesses:

Patrick McDonnell & Catherine Tighe

- o Catherine Tighe & John O'Neill – 4 Sep 1876 (Marriage, **St. Lawrence Parish** (RC))

Catherine Tighe (daughter):

Residence - 64 Sheriff Street - September 4, 1876

John O'Neill, son of John O'Neill & Jane Dunne (son-in-law):

Residence - 14 Mayor Street - September 4, 1876

Hurst

Wedding Witnesses:

Thomas Monks & Roseanne Dunne

- o Rachel Tighe & Thomas O'Halloran – 8 Mar 1877 (Marriage, **St. Lawrence Parish (RC)**)
  - ▪ Bridget Mary O'Halloran – b. 21 Jan 1878, bapt. 24 Jan 1878 (Baptism, **St. Lawrence Parish (RC)**)

Rachel Tighe (daughter):

Residence - 62 Sheriff Street - March 8, 1877

Thomas O'Halloran, son of Edward O'Halloran & Bridget Burns (son-in-law):

Residence - Drogheda - March 8, 1877

15 Emerald Street - January 24, 1878

- • Owen Tighe & Mary Unknown
  - o Catherine Tighe – bapt. 22 Jun 1746 (Baptism, **St. Catherine Parish (RC)**)
  - o Marcella Tighe – bapt. 10 Jul 1750 (Baptism, **St. Catherine Parish (RC)**)
  - o Charles Tighe – bapt. 2 Apr 1753 (Baptism, **St. Catherine Parish (RC)**)
- • Owen Tighe & Unknown
  - o Thomas Kelly Tighe & Catherine Brennan – 3 Feb 1882 (Marriage, **St. Andrew Parish (RC)**)

Thomas Kelly Tighe (son):

Residence - 13 Mayor Street - February 3, 1882

Catherine Brennan, daughter of Patrick Brennan (daughter-in-law):

Residence - 5 Clarence Place - February 3, 1882

Tighe Surname Ireland: 1600s to 1900s

- Patrick Tighe & Alice Byrne (B y r n e)

  o Hugh Tighe – b. 11 Apr 1862, bapt. 14 Apr 1862 (Baptism, **St. Nicholas Parish (RC)**)

  o Patrick Tighe – b. 19 May 1864, bapt. 23 May 1864 (Baptism, **St. Nicholas Parish (RC)**)

Patrick Tighe (father):

Residence - 58 Golden Lane - April 14, 1862

60 Golden Lane - May 23, 1864

- Patrick Tighe & Anne Geatley

  o Bridget Tighe – bapt. 5 May 1800 (Baptism, **St. Catherine Parish (RC)**)

  o Mary Tighe – bapt. 25 Mar 1804 (Baptism, **St. Catherine Parish (RC)**)

- Patrick Tighe & Bridget Coughlan

  o Christopher Tighe – bapt. 1834 (Baptism, **Clondalkin Parish (RC)**)

  o Mary Jane Tighe – bapt. 26 Mar 1836 (Baptism, **St. James Parish (RC)**)

  o Bridget Tighe – bapt. 9 Feb 1843 (Baptism, **St. James Parish (RC)**)

  o Margaret Tighe – bapt. 14 May 1847 (Baptism, **St. Nicholas Parish (RC)**)

  o Martin Tighe – bapt. 27 Jan 1850 (Baptism, **St. James Parish (RC)**)

Patrick Tighe (father):

Residence - 5th Lock - 1834

- Patrick Tighe & Bridget Foley

  o Patrick Tighe – b. 22 Jan 1882, bapt. 8 Feb 1882 (Baptism, **St. Mary, Pro Cathedral Parish (RC)**)

Hurst

Patrick Tighe (father):

Residence - 17 Gloucester Place - February 8, 1882

- Patrick Tighe & Bridget Polan

  - John Tighe – bapt. 24 Jun 1792 (Baptism, **St. Catherine Parish** (RC))

  - Catherine Tighe – bapt. 5 Aug 1802 (Baptism, **St. Catherine Parish** (RC))

  - Nicholas Tighe – bapt. 10 Sep 1804 (Baptism, **St. Catherine Parish** (RC))

- Patrick Tighe & Bridget Slevin

  - Bridget Tighe – bapt. 6 Nov 1834 (Baptism, **St. James Parish** (RC))

- Patrick Tighe & Bridget Tighe

  - John Tighe – bapt. 22 Aug 1832 (Baptism, **St. Mary, Pro Cathedral Parish** (RC))

- Patrick Tighe & Bridget Unknown

  - Thomas Joseph Tighe & Mary King – 1 Jul 1858 (Marriage, **St. Catherine Parish** (RC))

Thomas Joseph Tighe (son):

Residence - New Kilmainham - July 1, 1858

Mary King, daughter of Bernard King & Mary Unknown (daughter-in-law):

Residence - Corn Market - July 1, 1858

Wedding Witnesses:

Matthew Delahunty & Jane Tighe

- Patrick Tighe & Catherine Unknown

  - Unknown Tighe – bapt. 1807 (Baptism, **St. Andrew Parish** (RC))

  - Robert Tighe – bapt. 1810 (Baptism, **St. Andrew Parish** (RC))

  - Mary Tighe – bapt. 1813 (Baptism, **St. Andrew Parish** (RC))

- o Unknown Tighe – bapt. 1817 (Baptism, **St. Andrew Parish (RC)**)

- Patrick Tighe & Charlotte Tighe

  - o Margaret Tighe – b. 27 Apr 1897, bapt. 30 Apr 1897 (Baptism, **St. Audoen Parish**)

  - o Kathleen Christine Tighe – b. 8 Dec 1898, bapt. 8 Jan 1899 (Baptism, **St. Audoen Parish**)

  - o Grace Hamilton Tighe – b. 20 Mar 1902, bapt. 18 May 1902 (Baptism, **St. Audoen Parish**)

Patrick Tighe (father):

Residence - 17 Usher's Quay - April 27, 1897

January 8, 1899

17 St. Augustine Street - May 18, 1902

Occupation - Laborer - April 27, 1897

January 8, 1899

Workman - May 18, 1902

- Patrick Tighe & Eleanor Connor – 24 Oct 1802 (Marriage, **St. Andrew Parish (RC)**)

- Patrick Tighe & Eleanor Tighe – 14 Apr 1751 (Marriage, **St. Michan Parish (RC)**)

- Patrick Tighe & Jane Healy

  - o Mary Jane Tighe – b. 7 Nov 1869, bapt. 8 Nov 1869 (Baptism, **SS. Michael & John Parish (RC)**)

  - o Bridget Tighe – b. 25 Jan 1872, bapt. 29 Jan 1872 (Baptism, **SS. Michael & John Parish (RC)**)

Patrick Tighe (father):

Residence - 48 Georges Street - November 8, 1869

Hurst

4 Monks Court - January 29, 1872

- Patrick Tighe & Jane Unknown

    - Margaret Tighe – bapt. 30 Sep 1758 (Baptism, **St. Michan Parish** (RC))

- Patrick Tighe & Joan Unknown

    - Michael Tighe – b. 13 Jan 1864, bapt. 22 Jan 1864 (Baptism, **St. Michan Parish** (RC))

Patrick Tighe (father):

Residence - 2 Beresford Street - January 22, 1864

- Patrick Tighe & Margaret Byrne (B y r n e)

    - Catherine Tighe – b. 1880, bapt. 1880 (Baptism, **St. Andrew Parish** (RC))

    - Mary Tighe – b. 1881, bapt. 1881 (Baptism, **St. Andrew Parish** (RC))

    - Margaret Tighe – b. 1884, bapt. 1885 (Baptism, **St. Andrew Parish** (RC))

    - Agnes Tighe – b. 1887, bapt. 1887 (Baptism, **St. Andrew Parish** (RC))

Patrick Tighe (father):

Residence - 3 James Lane - 1880

2 James Lane - 1881

1884

4 James Lane - 1887

- Patrick Tighe & Margaret Keogh – 22 Jan 1849 (Marriage, **St. Michan Parish** (RC))

    - Mary Tighe – bapt. 12 Dec 1849 (Baptism, **St. Michan Parish** (RC))

    - James Tighe – bapt. 19 Apr 1852 (Baptism, **St. Michan Parish** (RC))

Tighe Surname Ireland: 1600s to 1900s

- Ellen Frances Tighe – b. 10 Mar 1854, bapt. 13 Mar 1854 (Baptism, **St. Mary, Pro Cathedral Parish (RC)**)

- Augustine William Tighe – b. 1857, bapt. 1857 (Baptism, **St. Andrew Parish (RC)**)

- Mary Catherine Tighe – b. 1859, bapt. 1859 (Baptism, **St. Andrew Parish (RC)**)

- Catherine Anne Tighe – b. 12 Mar 1863, bapt. 16 Mar 1863 (Baptism, **St. Mary, Pro Cathedral Parish (RC)**)

- Daniel Paul Tighe – b. 11 Jan 1865, bapt. 13 Jan 1865 (Baptism, **St. Mary, Pro Cathedral Parish (RC)**)

- Peter Tighe – b. 12 Jun 1867, bapt. 17 Jun 1867 (Baptism, **St. Mary, Pro Cathedral Parish (RC)**)

- Patrick John Tighe – b. 20 Jun 1870, bapt. 24 Jun 1870 (Baptism, **St. Mary, Pro Cathedral Parish (RC)**)

- Christopher William Tighe – b. 1873, bapt. 1873 (Baptism, **St. Andrew Parish (RC)**)

Patrick Tighe (father):

Residence - 13 Ryder's Row - March 13, 1854

Cuffe Street - 1859

45 Cole's Lane - March 16, 1863

June 17, 1867

44 Cole's Lane - January 13, 1865

44 Cabe Lane - June 24, 1870

2 Bowfow Row - 1873

Hurst

- Patrick Tighe & Margaret Reilly

  - Elizabeth Tighe – bapt. 21 Jan 1851 (Baptism, **St. Catherine Parish** (RC))

  - Mary Tighe – b. 14 Apr 1856, bapt. 25 Apr 1856 (Baptism, **St. Nicholas Parish** (RC))

Patrick Tighe (father):

Residence - 6 Plunket Street - April 25, 1856

- Patrick Tighe & Margaret Unknown

  - Elizabeth Tighe – bapt. 28 Nov 1745 (Baptism, **St. Mary, Pro Cathedral Parish** (RC))

- Patrick Tighe & Mary Connolly

  - Bridget Tighe – bapt. 1819 (Baptism, **St. Mary Parish** (RC))

- Patrick Tighe & Mary Murphy – 18 Jun 1843 (Marriage, **St. Andrew Parish** (RC))

  - John Tighe – bapt. 12 Apr 1844 (Baptism, **St. James Parish** (RC))

  - David Philip Tighe – bapt. 2 Nov 1845 (Baptism, **St. James Parish** (RC))

  - Patrick Tighe – bapt. 29 Aug 1847 (Baptism, **St. James Parish** (RC))

  - William Tighe – bapt. 6 Apr 1851 (Baptism, **St. James Parish** (RC))

  - Joseph Tighe – bapt. 11 Apr 1853 (Baptism, **St. James Parish** (RC))

  - James Tighe – bapt. 28 Sep 1854 (Baptism, **St. James Parish** (RC))

  - Anne Tighe – bapt. 22 Apr 1856 (Baptism, **St. James Parish** (RC))

  - Edward Tighe – b. 27 Aug 1857, bapt. 20 Sep 1857 (Baptism, **St. James Parish** (RC))

Patrick Tighe (father):

Residence - Golden Bridge - September 28, 1854

April 22, 1856

2nd Lock, Grand Canal - September 20, 1857

Tighe Surname Ireland: 1600s to 1900s

- Patrick Tighe & Mary Nowdes – 14 Sep 1783 (Marriage, **St. Michan Parish** (RC))

  o Arthur Tighe – bapt. 16 Sep 1784 (Baptism, **St. Michan Parish** (RC))

  o James Tighe – bapt. 5 Dec 1785 (Baptism, **St. Michan Parish** (RC))

  o Patrick Tighe – bapt. 18 Mar 1787 (Baptism, **St. Michan Parish** (RC))

  o Elizabeth Tighe – bapt. 22 May 1788 (Baptism, **St. Michan Parish** (RC))

  o Edmund Tighe – bapt. 4 Jun 1789 (Baptism, **St. Michan Parish** (RC))

  o Mary Anne Tighe – bapt. 8 Aug 1790 (Baptism, **St. Michan Parish** (RC))

  o Walter Tighe – bapt. 2 Sep 1791 (Baptism, **St. Michan Parish** (RC))

- Patrick Tighe & Sarah McClusky

  o John Tighe – bapt. 22 Aug 1842 (Baptism, **St. Nicholas Parish** (RC))

- Patrick Tighe & Susan Lee

  o Mary Tighe – bapt. 24 Mar 1829 (Baptism, **St. Catherine Parish** (RC))

  o Susan Tighe, bapt. 27 Aug 1839 (Baptism, **St. Catherine Parish** (RC)) & John Watson – 10 Feb 1861 (Marriage, **St. Michan Parish** (RC))

    ▪ Mary Clare Watson – b. 11 Dec 1861, bapt. 16 Dec 1861 (Baptism, **St. Michan Parish** (RC))

    ▪ Anne Watson, b. 10 Nov 1863, bapt. 16 Nov 1863 (Baptism, **St. Mary, Pro Cathedral Parish** (RC)) & Michael Cleary – 25 Nov 1883 (Marriage, **St. Mary, Pro Cathedral Parish** (RC))

Anne Watson (daughter):

Residence - 15 Ryder's Row - November 25, 1883

Michael Cleary, son of John Cleary & Frances Russell (son-in-law):

Residence - 33 Stafford Street - November 25, 1883

Hurst

Wedding Witnesses:

Richard Murray & Catherine Watson

- Catherine Watson – b. 17 Nov 1865, bapt. 20 Nov 1865 (Baptism, **St. Mary, Pro Cathedral Parish** (RC))

- Edward John Watson – b. 25 Jun 1868, bapt. 6 Jul 1868 (Baptism, **St. Michan Parish** (RC))

- Patrick Joseph Watson – b. 25 May 1870, bapt. 1 Jun 1870 (Baptism, **St. Michan Parish** (RC))

- John Watson – b. 24 Jun 1872, bapt. 26 Jun 1872 (Baptism, **St. Michan Parish** (RC))

- Edward Watson – b. 31 Oct 1874, bapt. 6 Nov 1874 (Baptism, **St. Michan Parish** (RC))

- Patrick Joseph Watson – b. 19 May 1878, bapt. 22 May 1878 (Baptism, **St. Mary, Pro Cathedral Parish** (RC))

- John Michael Watson – b. 2 Oct 1880, bapt. 4 Oct 1880 (Baptism, **St. Mary, Pro Cathedral Parish** (RC))

Susan Tighe (daughter):

Residence - 17 Greek Street - February 10, 1861

John Watson, son of Edward Watson & Jane Unknown (son-in-law):

Residence - 9 Greek Street - February 10, 1861

Beresford Street - December 16, 1861

31 Moore Street - November 16, 1863

45 Great Britain Street - November 20, 1865

134 Upper Dorset Street - July 6, 1868

Tighe Surname Ireland: 1600s to 1900s

134 Dorset Street - June 1, 1870

12 Linenhall Street - June 26, 1872

20 Charles Street - November 6, 1874

117 Capel Street - May 22, 1878

15 Ryder's Row - October 4, 1880

- Patrick Tighe & Unknown
  - Jane Tighe – bapt. 12 May 1698 (Baptism, **St. Patrick Parish**)
- Patrick Tighe & Unknown
  - Anne Tighe & Patrick O'Keefe – 8 Nov 1868 (Marriage, **St. James Parish** (RC))
    - James Patrick O'Keefe – b. 1872, bapt. 1872 (Baptism, **St. Andrew Parish** (RC))
    - John Joseph O'Keefe – b. 21 Oct 1888, bapt. 28 Oct 1888 (Baptism, **St. Joseph Parish** (RC))

Anne Tighe (daughter):

Residence - Kilmainham - November 8, 1868

Patrick O'Keefe, son of James O'Keefe (son-in-law):

Residence - Kilmainham - November 8, 1868

3 Great Clarence Street - 1872

Harold's Cross Road - October 28, 1888

Wedding Witnesses:

Thomas Doyle & Mayanite (Possibly Mary Anne) Tighe

Hurst

o   Mary Tighe & Lawrence O'Toole – 22 May 1869 (Marriage, **St. James Parish** (RC))

Mary Tighe (daughter):

Residence - Kilmainham - May 22, 1869

Lawrence O'Toole, son of Patrick O'Toole (son-in-law):

Residence - Curryhill, Co. Kildare - May 22, 1869

Wedding Witnesses:

Gulielmo O'Connor & Margaret Tighe

o   Margaret Tighe & John Cerlin – 28 Aug 1871 (Marriage, **St. James Parish** (RC))

Margaret Tighe (daughter):

Residence - Kilmainham - August 28, 1871

John Cerlin, son of Gulielmo Cerlin (son-in-law):

Residence - Kilkenny - August 28, 1871

- Patrick Tighe & Unknown
  - Mary Tighe & James P. Murphy – 13 Nov 1873 (Marriage, **St. James Parish** (RC))
    - Margaret Mary Murphy – b. 9 Jan 1877, bapt. 23 Jan 1877 (Baptism, **St. James Parish** (RC))

Mary Tighe (daughter):

Residence - 2nd Lock, Grand Canal - November 13, 1873

James P. Murphy, son of Anthony Murphy (son-in-law):

Residence - 4 Salin Terrace, South Circular Road - November 13, 1873

Tighe Surname Ireland: 1600s to 1900s

2nd Lock, Gran Canal - January 23, 1877

Wedding Witnesses:

Joseph Tighe & Teresa Duggan

- Peter Tighe & Elizabeth Unknown

  o   Peter Tighe – bapt. 1771 (Baptism, **St. Andrew Parish** (RC))

- Peter Tighe & Jane Unknown

  o   James Tighe – bapt. 1818 (Baptism, **Clondalkin Parish** (RC))

- Peter Tighe & Mary Kelly

  o   Elizabeth Tighe – bapt. 1812 (Baptism, **Clondalkin Parish** (RC))

  o   Anne Tighe – bapt. 1816 (Baptism, **Clondalkin Parish** (RC))

- Philip Tighe & Anne Unknown

  o   William Tighe – bapt. Jan 1799 (Baptism, **St. Mary, Pro Cathedral Parish** (RC))

- Philip Tighe & Dorothy Smothers

  o   John Tighe – b. 21 Nov 1856, bapt. 24 Nov 1856 (Baptism, **St. Nicholas Parish** (RC))

  o   Mary Tighe – b. 22 Dec 1859, bapt. 23 Dec 1859 (Baptism, **St. Nicholas Parish** (RC))

Philip Tighe (father):

Residence - 48 Patrick Street - November 24, 1856

83 Francis Street - December 23, 1859

- Richard Tighe, bur. 29 Mar 1725 (Burial, **St. Catherine Parish**) & Dorothy Tighe

  o   Mable Tighe – bapt. 21 Dec 1719 (Baptism, **St. Catherine Parish**)

  o   Anne Tighe – bapt. 25 Jan 1720 (Baptism, **St. Catherine Parish**)

  o   Dorothy Tighe – bapt. 7 Feb 1722 (Baptism, **St. Catherine Parish**)

Hurst

Richard Tighe (father):

Occupation - Esquire - December 21, 1719

January 25, 1720

- Richard Tighe & Elizabeth Unknown

  o Richard Tighe – bapt. 28 Jul 1786 (Baptism, St. Catherine Parish (RC))

- Richard Tighe, bur. 4 May 1699 (Burial, St. Michan Parish) & Mabel Tighe

  o Richard Tighe – bapt. 2 May 1678 (Baptism, St. Michan Parish)

  o William Tighe – bapt. 17 Jul 1681 (Baptism, St. Michan Parish), bur. 19 Jul 1681 (Burial, St. Michan Parish)

  o Richard Tighe – bapt. 14 Aug 1682 (Baptism, St. Michan Parish)

  o William Tighe – bapt. 10 Jan 1684 (Baptism, St. Michan Parish)

  o Robert Tighe – bapt. 7 May 1686 (Baptism, St. Michan Parish)

  o Mary Tighe – bapt. 5 Aug 1687 (Baptism, St. Michan Parish)

  o John Tighe – bapt. 19 Dec 1688 (Baptism, St. Michan Parish), bur. 24 Sep 1689 (Burial, St. Michan Parish)

  o Sterne (S t e r n e) Tighe – bapt. 21 Jan 1690 (Baptism, St. Michan Parish)

  o Stephen Tighe – bapt. 16 May 1694 (Baptism, St. Michan Parish), bur. 17 Dec 1698 (Burial, St. Michan Parish)

Richard Tighe (father):

Occupation - Gentleman - May 2, 1678

July 17, 1681

August 14, 1682

Tighe Surname Ireland: 1600s to 1900s

January 10, 1684

May 7, 1686

August 5, 1687

December 19, 1688

January 21, 1690

May 16, 1694

May 4, 1699

- Richard Tighe & Mary Tighe, bur. 18 Apr 1677 (Burial, **St. Michan Parish**)

- Richard Tighe & Mary Unknown

    o   Richard Tighe – bapt. 4 Sep 1758 (Baptism, **St. Michan Parish (RC)**)

- Richard Tighe & Unknown

    o   Arabella Tighe, b. 1836 & Joseph Randall – 3 Nov 1856 (Marriage, **St. Anne Parish**)

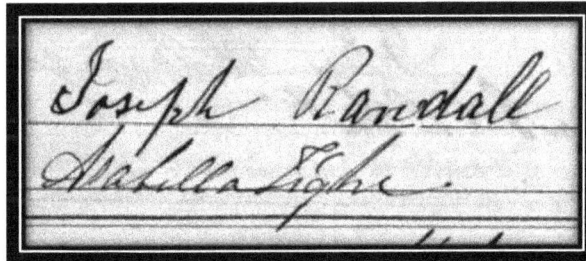

Signatures:

Arabella Tighe (daughter):

Residence - 10 South Anne Street - November 3, 1856

Age at Marriage - 20 years

Hurst

Joseph Randall, son of Edwin Randall (son-in-law):

Residence - 10 South Anne Street - November 3, 1856

Occupation - Servant - November 3, 1856

Edwin Randall (father):

Occupation - Game Keeper

Richard Tighe (father):

Occupation - Shoemaker

Wedding Witnesses:

William Drury & Mary Sawlon

Signatures:

- Richard Tighe & Unknown
  - Edward Tighe & Susan Louisa Gorges – 18 Apr 1861 (Marriage, St. Peter Parish)

Signatures:

Tighe Surname Ireland: 1600s to 1900s

Edward Tighe (son):

    Residence - 46 Lower Leeson Street - April 18, 1861

    Occupation - Esquire - April 18, 1861

    Relationship Status at Marriage - widow

Susan Louisa Gorges, daughter of John Gorges (daughter-in-law):

    Residence - Miltown - April 18, 1861

John Gorges (father):

    Occupation - Clerk in Holy Orders

Richard Tighe (father):

    Occupation - Esquire

Wedding Witnesses:

William Gorges & R. H. Gorges

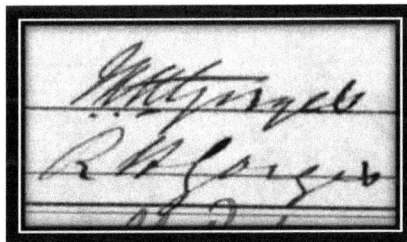

Signatures:

- Richard Tighe & Unknown

  - Emma Jane Tighe & Vesey Francis Bashford – 19 Dec 1889 (Marriage, **St. Stephen Parish**)

Signatures:

Emma Jane Tighe (daughter):

   Residence - 7 Holles Street - December 19, 1889

Vesey Francis Bashford, son of James Bashford (son-in-law):

   Residence - King's Court, Co. Cavan - December 19, 1889

   Occupation - Game Keeper - December 19, 1889

James Bashford (father):

   Occupation - Esquire

Richard Tighe (father):

   Occupation - Farmer

Tighe Surname Ireland: 1600s to 1900s

Wedding Witnesses:

Elizabeth Sharpe & Emily C. Bashford

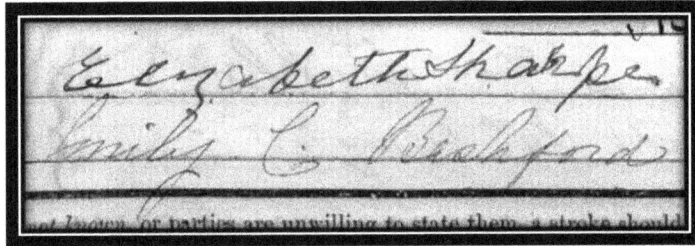

Signatures:

- Richard Philip Tighe & Mary Anne Tighe

  o Edward Robert Tighe – bapt. 23 Jul 1842 (Baptism, **St. George Parish**)

Richard Philip Tighe (father):

Residence - No. 20 Middle Gardiner's Street - July 23, 1842

Occupation - Solicitor - July 23, 1842

- Robert Tighe & Catherine Unknown

  o Thomas Tighe & Mary Antoinette Dolphin – 29 Apr 1875 (Marriage, **St. Andrew Parish (RC)**)

    ▪ Thomas Peter Joseph Aloysius Tighe – b. 1876, bapt. 1876 (Baptism, **St. Andrew Parish (RC)**)

Thomas Tighe (son):

Residence - The Heath, Co. Mayo - April 29, 1875

8 Leinster Street - 1876

Hurst

Mary Antoinette Dolphin, daughter of Peter Dolphin & Antoinette Unknown

(daughter-in-law):

Residence - Danes Fort, Galway - April 29, 1875

- Robert Tighe & Mary Barry
  - Mary Tighe – b. 15 Jul 1862, bapt. 31 Jul 1862 (Baptism, **St. James Parish** (RC))

Robert Tighe (father):

Residence - 13 Bow Lane - July 31, 1862

- Robert Tighe & Mary Clemments – 6 Aug 1715 (Marriage, **St. Michan Parish**)

Robert Tighe (husband):

Occupation - Gentleman - August 6, 1715

- Robert Tighe & Mary Stretch
  - John Joseph Tighe – b. 14 Nov 1875, bapt. 24 Nov 1875 (Baptism, **St. Lawrence Parish** (RC))
  - Mary Tighe – b. 20 Aug 1877, bapt. 24 Aug 1877 (Baptism, **St. Mary, Pro Cathedral Parish** (RC))
  - Patrick Tighe – 18 Nov 1879, bapt. 21 Nov 1879 (Baptism, **St. Mary, Pro Cathedral Parish** (RC))
  - Susan Jane Tighe – b. 10 Apr 1882, bapt. 12 Apr 1882 (Baptism, **St. Mary, Pro Cathedral Parish** (RC))
  - Peter Michael Tighe – b. 29 Jun 1884, bapt. 30 Jun 1884 (Baptism, **St. Mary, Pro Cathedral Parish** (RC))

- o Bridget Tighe – b. 12 Jul 1886, bapt. 16 Jul 1886 (Baptism, **St. Mary, Pro Cathedral Parish** (RC))
- o Catherine Christine Tighe – b. 8 Dec 1887, bapt. 12 Dec 1887 (Baptism, **St. Mary, Pro Cathedral Parish** (RC))

Robert Tighe (father):

Residence - 49 Sheriff Street - November 24, 1875

> **18 Lower Buckingham Street - August 24, 1877**

> **18 Buckingham Place - November 21, 1879**

> **18 Buckingham Street - April 12, 1882**

> **9 Upper Buckingham Street - June 30, 1884**

> **December 12, 1887**

> **9 Bailey's Row off Summer Hill - July 16, 1886**

- • Robert Tighe & Mary Unknown
  - o Sophie Tighe – bapt. 14 Apr 1786 (Baptism, **St. Catherine Parish**)

Robert Tighe (father):

Residence - Barrack Street - April 14, 1786

- • Robert Tighe & Mary Unknown
  - o Patrick Tighe & Julie Sheridan – 8 Jul 1888 (Marriage, **St. Mary, Haddington Road Parish** (RC))
    - ▪ Mary Bridget Tighe – b. 20 Apr 1889, bapt. 6 May 1889 (Baptism, **St. Mary, Haddington Road Parish** (RC))

Hurst

Patrick Tighe (son):

Residence - Thornfield, Donnybrook - July 8, 1888

8 Mespil Terrace - May 6, 1889

Julia Sheridan, daughter of Thomas Sheridan & Anne Unknown (daughter-in-law):

Residence - 71 Haddington Road - July 8, 1888

- Robert Tighe & Mary Anne Moore

  o Robert Tighe – b. 1 Jun 1886, bapt. 4 Jun 1886 (Baptism, **St. Audoen Parish** (RC))

  o Christopher Tighe – b. 22 Dec 1888, bapt. 28 Dec 1888 (Baptism, **St. Audoen Parish** (RC))

Robert Tighe (father):

Residence - 20 Cook Street - June 1, 1886

21 Cook Street - December 28, 1888

- Robert Tighe & Unknown

  o Robert Tighe & Hester Catherine Smith – 23 Nov 1847 (Marriage, **St. Peter Parish**)

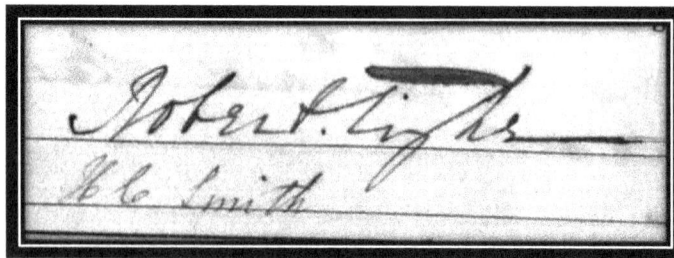

Signatures:

Robert Tighe (son):

Residence - 16 Fitzwilliam Square - November 23, 1847

Occupation - Barrister at Law - November 23, 1847

98

Hester Catherine Smith, daughter of Thomas Berry Cusack Smith

(daughter-in-law):

> Residence - Merrion Square East - November 23, 1847

Thomas Berry Cusack Smith (father):

> Occupation - Master of the Rolls in Ireland

Robert Tighe (father):

> Occupation - Gentleman

Wedding Witnesses:

T. M. Smith & Montague Chapman

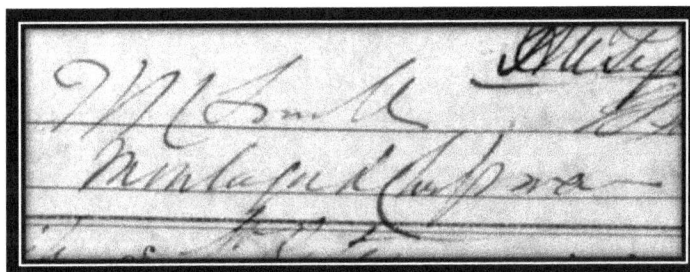

Signatures:

- Robert Tighe & Unknown
  - Francis Tighe & Catherine Fitzsimons – 27 Oct 1881 (Marriage, St. Agatha Parish (RC))
    - Catherine Mary Tighe – b. 20 Apr 1884, bapt. 25 Apr 1884 (Baptism, St. Agatha Parish (RC))

Francis Tighe (son):

Residence - 32 Glengariffe Parade - October 27, 1881

22 Portland Street - April 25, 1884

Hurst

Catherine Fitzsimons, daughter of Bernard Fitzsimons (daughter-in-law):

Residence - 9 Portland Street - October 27, 1881

- Samuel Tighe & Unknown
  - Thomas Tighe & Mary O'Donnell – 2 Apr 1855 (Marriage, **St. Paul Parish**)

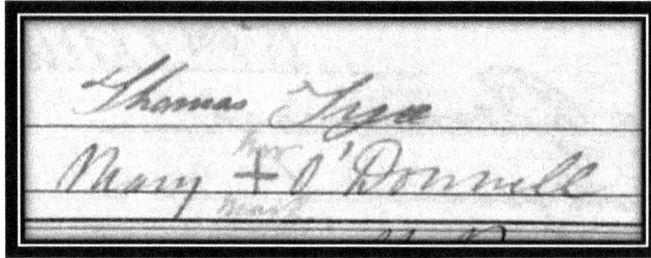

Signatures:

Thomas Tighe (son):

Residence - Linen Hall Barracks - April 2, 1855

Occupation - Sergeant 48th Regiment Militia - April 2, 1855

Mary O'Donnell, daughter of Neil O'Donnell (daughter-in-law):

Residence - Liffey Street - April 2, 1855

Occupation - Laundress - April 2, 1855

Neil O'Donnell (father):

Occupation - Shepherd

Samuel Tighe (father):

Occupation - Carpenter

Tighe Surname Ireland: 1600s to 1900s

Wedding Witnesses:

Richard Morton & Sarah Olgard

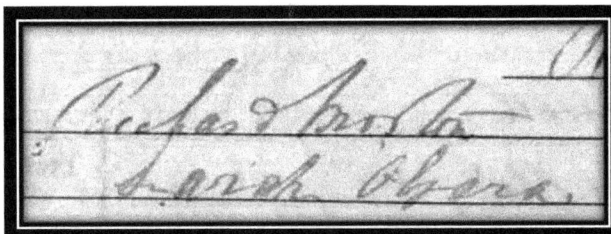

Signatures:

- Sterne (S t e r n e) Tighe & Abigail Ward – 31 Dec 1763 (Marriage, **St. Michael Parish**)

Sterne Tighe (husband):

Occupation - Gentleman - December 31, 1763

- Sterne (S t e r n e) Tighe & Anne Tighe

  - Margaret Barbara Tighe – bapt. 27 Sep 1802 (Baptism, **St. George Parish**)

- Sterne (S t e r n e) Tighe & Dorothy Blundell – 28 Feb 1716 (Marriage, **St. Michan Parish**)

  - Richard Tighe – bapt. 7 Feb 1727 (Baptism, **St. Audoen Parish**)

  - Stearn (S t e a r n) Tighe – bapt. 15 Jul 1733 (Baptism, **St. Audoen Parish**)

  - Cordelia Tighe – bapt. 28 Jun 1736 (Baptism, **St. Audoen Parish**)

  - Martha Tighe – bapt. 28 Jun 1736 (Baptism, **St. Audoen Parish**)

  - William Tighe – bapt. 14 Jun 1741 (Baptism, **St. Audoen Parish**)

Sterne Tighe (father):

Occupation - Merchant - February 28, 1716

- Thomas Tighe & Alice Hatch

  - Michael Tighe – b. 1863, bapt. 1863 (Baptism, **St. Andrew Parish (RC)**)

Hurst

- o Patrick Tighe – b. 16 Mar 1865, bapt. 20 Mar 1865 (Baptism, **St. Mary, Pro Cathedral Parish** (RC))

- o Mary Tighe, b. 1867, bapt. 1867 (Baptism, **Clondalkin Parish** (RC)) & Thomas Mohan – 28 Aug 1887 (Marriage, **St. Mary, Pro Cathedral Parish** (RC))

  - Patrick Joseph Mohan – b. 12 May 1889, bapt. 13 May 1889 (Baptism, **St. Mary, Pro Cathedral Parish** (RC))

  - Thomas Valentine Mohan – b. 15 Feb 1891, bapt. 18 Feb 1891 (Baptism, **St. Mary, Pro Cathedral Parish** (RC))

  - Michael Christopher Mohan – b. 22 Nov 1892, bapt. 28 Nov 1892 (Baptism, **St. Mary, Pro Cathedral Parish** (RC))

  - Alice Mary Mohan – b. 6 Aug 1894, bapt. 13 Aug 1894 (Baptism, **St. Mary, Pro Cathedral Parish** (RC))

  - Edward Joseph Mohan – b. 3 Mar 1897, bapt. 9 Mar 1897 (Baptism, **St. Mary, Pro Cathedral Parish** (RC))

  - Anne Christine Mohan – b. 23 Dec 1899, bapt. 27 Dec 1899 (Baptism, **St. Mary, Pro Cathedral Parish** (RC))

Mary Tighe (daughter):

Residence - 66 Lower Mecklenburgh Street - August 28, 1887

Thomas Mohan, son of Edward Mohan & Mary A. Hobson (son-in-law):

Residence - 69 Montgomery Street - August 28, 1887

48 and 44 Lower Tyrone Street - May 13, 1889

50 Tyrone Street - February 18, 1891

Tighe Surname Ireland: 1600s to 1900s

5 George's Place - November 28, 1892

21 George's Place - August 13, 1894

13 George's Place - March 9, 1897

17 George's Place - December 27, 1899

Thomas Tighe (father):

Residence - 5 Sandwich Place - 1863

36 Lower Mecklenburgh Street - March 20, 1865

Chapelizod - 1867

- Thomas Tighe & Alice Unknown

  o Judith Tighe – bapt. 7 Nov 1754 (Baptism, **St. Michan Parish** (RC))

- Thomas Tighe & Alice Unknown

  o Joseph Tighe – bapt. 10 Sep 1849 (Baptism, **St. James Parish** (RC))

- Thomas Tighe & Anne Brady

  o Elizabeth Tighe – bapt. 10 May 1778 (Baptism, **St. Catherine Parish** (RC))

  o Catherine Tighe – bapt. 29 Apr 1787 (Baptism, **St. Catherine Parish** (RC))

- Thomas Tighe & Anne Reilly

  o Rose Tighe – bapt. 17 Jul 1780 (Baptism, **St. Catherine Parish** (RC))

- Thomas Tighe & Anne Unknown

  o Daniel Tighe – bapt. 5 Sep 1784 (Baptism, **St. Catherine Parish** (RC))

- Thomas Tighe & Anne Unknown

  o Hugh Tighe & Bridget Kelly – 16 May 1870 (Marriage, **St. Nicholas Parish** (RC))

Hurst

Hugh Tighe (son):

Residence - 143 King Street - May 16, 1870

Bridget Kelly, daughter of Charles Kelly & Catherine Unknown (daughter-in-law):

Residence - 51 New Street - May 16, 1870

- Thomas Tighe & Anne Watson

  o Anne Tighe – bapt. 3 Feb 1848 (Baptism, **St. James Parish** (RC))

  o Thomas Tighe – bapt. 22 Dec 1851 (Baptism, **St. James Parish** (RC))

  o Patrick Tighe – b. 18 Nov 1857, bapt. 19 Nov 1857 (Baptism, **St. James Parish** (RC))

  o Mary Tighe – b. 15 Apr 1860, bapt. 16 Apr 1860 (Baptism, **St. James Parish** (RC))

  o Christopher Tighe – b. 24 Nov 1861, bapt. 28 Nov 1861 (Baptism, **St. James Parish** (RC))

Thomas Tighe (father):

Residence - Inchicore - April 16, 1860

Black Lion - November 19, 1857

November 28, 1861

- Thomas Tighe & Barbara Tighe – 15 Sep 1835 (Marriage, **St. Peter Parish**)

Thomas Tighe (husband):

Residence - Pembroke Road - September 15, 1835

Barbara Tighe (wife):

Residence - Newtown Mount Kennedy, Newcastle Co. Wicklow -

September 15, 1835

Tighe Surname Ireland: 1600s to 1900s

- Thomas Tighe & Bridget Unknown

  o Bridget Tighe – bapt. 7 May 1824 (Baptism, **St. Mary, Pro Cathedral Parish (RC)**)

Thomas Tighe (father):

Residence - Abbey Street - May 7, 1824

- Thomas Tighe & Catherine Farrell

  o Bridget Tighe – bapt. 6 Jun 1773 (Baptism, **St. Nicholas Parish (RC)**)

- Thomas Tighe & Elizabeth Doyle

  o Hubert Tighe – b. 30 Jul 1863, bapt. 4 Aug 1863 (Baptism, **St. Catherine Parish (RC)**)

  o Elizabeth Tighe – b. 15 Jan 1866, bapt. 26 Jan 1866 (Baptism, **St. Michan Parish (RC)**)

Thomas Tighe (father):

Residence - 3 Bonham Street - August 4, 1863

6 Church Street - January 26, 1866

- Thomas Tighe & Elizabeth Unknown

  o Elizabeth Tighe – bapt. 28 Apr 1756 (Baptism, **St. Michan Parish (RC)**)

- Thomas Tighe & Elizabeth Margaret Tighe

  o Emily Henrietta Tighe – bapt. 7 Oct 1825 (Baptism, **St. Mark Parish**), bur. 10 Mar 1826

    (Burial, **St. Mark Parish**)

Emily Henrietta Tighe (daughter):

Residence - Erne Street - before March 10, 1826

Age at Death - 6 months

Hurst

- Thomas Tighe & Jane Condron

  o Mary Tighe – b. 16 Nov 1869, bapt. 24 Nov 1869 (Baptism, **St. Michan Parish (RC)**)

  o James Joseph Tighe – b. 21 Sep 1871, bapt. 25 Sep 1871 (Baptism, **St. Michan Parish (RC)**)

  o Catherine Tighe – b. 22 Sep 1873, bapt. 24 Sep 1873 (Baptism, **St. Michan Parish (RC)**)

Thomas Tighe (father):

Residence - 29 Nelson Street - November 24, 1869

Flynn's Cottages Cross Guns - September 25, 1871

Flynn's Cottage - September 24, 1873

- Thomas Tighe & Jane Kehoe – 22 Jul 1827 (Marriage, **St. Andrew Parish (RC)**)

  o John Tighe – bapt. 1828 (Baptism, **St. Andrew Parish (RC)**)

  o Joan Tighe – bapt. Apr 1835 (Baptism, **St. Michan Parish (RC)**)

  o Mary Tighe – bapt. 1838 (Baptism, **St. Andrew Parish (RC)**)

  o Harriet Tighe – bapt. 1840 (Baptism, **St. Andrew Parish (RC)**)

  o Thomas Tighe – bapt. 28 Mar 1841 (Baptism, **Rathmines Parish (RC)**)

  o Robert Patrick Tighe – bapt. 1843 (Baptism, **St. Andrew Parish (RC)**)

- Thomas Tighe & Jane Nolan – 18 Feb 1833 (Marriage, **St. Nicholas Parish (RC)**)

- Thomas Tighe & Jane Shannon

  o John Tighe – bapt. 18 Dec 1833 (Baptism, **St. Nicholas Parish (RC)**)

  o Timothy Tighe, bapt. 9 Dec 1835 (Baptism, **St. Nicholas Parish (RC)**) & Elizabeth O'Brien

    – 14 Apr 1868 (Marriage, **St. Nicholas Parish (RC)**)

    ▪ Alphonse Michael Tighe – b. 29 Apr 1868, bapt. 11 May 1868 (Baptism, **St. Nicholas Parish (RC)**)

Tighe Surname Ireland: 1600s to 1900s

- Timothy Joseph Tighe – b. 4 May 1870, bapt. 9 May 1870 (Baptism, **St. Nicholas Parish** (RC))

- Mary Elizabeth Tighe – b. 1874, bapt. 1874 (Baptism, **St. Andrew Parish** (RC))

- Francis Dominick Tighe – b. 1876, bapt. 1876 (Baptism, **St. Andrew Parish** (RC))

Timothy Tighe (son):

Residence - 20 Wood Street - April 14, 1868

May 11, 1868

6 Mark's Alley - May 9, 1870

19 King Street - 1874

19 South King Street - 1876

Elizabeth O'Brien, daughter of Thomas O'Brien & Mary Unknown (daughter-in-law):

Residence- 20 Wood Street - April 14, 1868

Wedding Witnesses:

Edward Sherwood & Mary O'Brien

- ○ Elizabeth Tighe – bapt. 2 Jun 1837 (Baptism, **St. Nicholas Parish** (RC))

- ○ Michael Tighe – bapt. 26 Jun 1839 (Baptism, **St. Nicholas Parish** (RC))

- ○ Timothy Tighe – bapt. 18 Apr 1843 (Baptism, **St. Michan Parish** (RC))

- Thomas Tighe & Jane Unknown

- ○ James Tighe – bapt. 21 Jul 1830 (Baptism, **St. Mary, Pro Cathedral Parish** (RC))

- Thomas Tighe & Jane Unknown

- ○ Thomas Tighe & Margaret Curran – 12 Apr 1863 (Marriage, **St. Michan Parish** (RC))

Hurst

Thomas Tighe (son):

Residence - 67 Wellington Street - April 12, 1863

Margaret Curran, daughter of Michael Curran & Margaret Unknown

(daughter-in-law):

Residence - 67 Wellington Street - April 12, 1863

Wedding Witnesses:

Thomas Tighe & Elizabeth Hynes

- Thomas Tighe & Kathleen Freston
  - Dorothy Eleanor Tighe – b. 1899, bapt. 1899 (Baptism, **St. Andrew Parish** (RC))

Thomas Tighe (father):

Residence - Ballyjones - 1899

- Thomas Tighe & Margaret Kiernan (K i e r n a n)
  - Thomas Tighe – bapt. 20 Feb 1855 (Baptism, **SS. Michael & John Parish** (RC))
  - John Joseph Tighe – b. 24 Feb 1858, bapt. 2 Mar 1858 (Baptism, **SS. Michael & John Parish** (RC))

Thomas Tighe (father):

Residence - 9 Winetavern Street - March 2, 1858

- Thomas Tighe & Margaret McGuinness
  - Margaret Tighe – bapt. 9 Sep 1883 (Baptism, **SS. Michael & John Parish** (RC))

Tighe Surname Ireland: 1600s to 1900s

Margaret Tighe (daughter):

Remarks about Birth - died

- Thomas Tighe & Mary Holland

  o Felix Tighe – bapt. 31 May 1813 (Baptism, **St. James Parish (RC)**)

- Thomas Tighe & Mary McConnell or O'Connor

  o Thomas Christopher Tighe – b. 20 Nov 1864, bapt. 30 Nov 1864 (Baptism, **St. Michan Parish (RC)**)

  o Jane Tighe – b. 11 Oct 1866, bapt. 17 Oct 1866 (Baptism, **St. Michan Parish (RC)**)

Thomas Tighe (father):

Residence - 7 Henrietta Place - November 30, 1864

October 17, 1866

- Thomas Tighe & Mary Newton – 14 Jan 1816 (Marriage, **St. Andrew Parish (RC)**)

  o Alice Tighe – bapt. 1817 (Baptism, **St. Andrew Parish (RC)**)

- Thomas Tighe & Mary Tighe

  o Anne Tighe – bapt. 16 Nov 1835 (Baptism, **St. Mary, Pro Cathedral Parish (RC)**)

- Thomas Tighe & Mary Unknown

  o Mary Anne Tighe – bapt. 1819 (Baptism, **St. Andrew Parish (RC)**)

  o Catherine Tighe – bapt. 1820 (Baptism, **St. Andrew Parish (RC)**)

- Thomas Tighe & Mary Unknown

  o Mary Tighe – bapt. 26 Mar 1820 (Baptism, **St. James Parish (RC)**)

- Thomas Tighe & Mary Unknown

  o Elizabeth Tighe – bapt. Jan 1843 (Baptism, **SS. Michael & John Parish (RC)**)

  o John Tighe – bapt. 26 Aug 1845 (Baptism, **SS. Michael & John Parish (RC)**)

- Thomas Tighe & Mary Unknown

  o Thomas Tighe & Mary Coffey – 1 Jul 1883 (Marriage, **St. Michan Parish (RC)**)

    ▪ Thomas Tighe – b. 13 Oct 1884, bapt. 22 Oct 1884 (Baptism, **St. Michan Parish (RC)**)

    ▪ Christopher Tighe – b. 25 Dec 1886, bapt. 5 Jan 1887 (Baptism, **St. Michan Parish (RC)**)

Thomas Tighe (son):

Residence - 4 Bull Lane - July 1, 1883

> **5 Beef Row - October 22, 1884**

> **52 Mary's Lane - January 5, 1887**

Mary Coffey, daughter of Bartholomew Coffey & Mary Unknown

(daughter-in-law):

Residence - 4 Bull Lane - July 1, 1883

- Thomas Tighe & Susan Unknown

  o Thomas Tighe – bapt. 14 Jul 1793 (Baptism, **St. Audoen Parish (RC)**)

- Thomas Tighe & Teresa Breslin

  o Thomas J. Tighe – bapt. 6 Dec 1852 (Baptism, **St. Michan Parish (RC)**)

- Thomas Tighe & Teresa Unknown

  o Mary Tighe – bapt. 23 Mar 1855 (Baptism, **St. Audoen Parish (RC)**)

Tighe Surname Ireland: 1600s to 1900s

- Thomas Tighe & Unknown

  o Thomas Tighe & Margaret Blevins – 2 Sep 1852 (Marriage, **St. Peter Parish**)

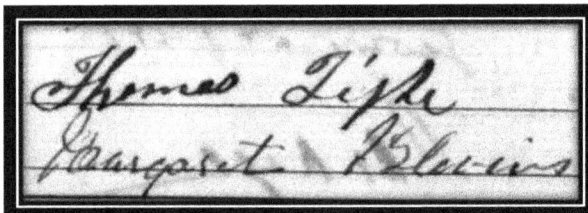

Signatures:

  - James Henry Tighe – b. 22 Jun 1853, bapt. 25 Jul 1853 (Baptism, **St. Peter Parish**)

  - Thomas John Tighe – b. 6 Jun 1854, bapt. 24 Dec 1854 (Baptism, **St. Peter Parish**)

  - Margaret Catherine Tighe – b. 4 Jan 1857, bapt. 15 Feb 1857 (Baptism, **St. Peter Parish**)

  - Robert Richard Tighe – b. 8 Nov 1859, bapt. 12 Feb 1860 (Baptism, **St. Peter Parish**)

  - William Edward Tighe – b. 12 Apr 1862, bapt. 1 Jun 1862 (Baptism, **St. Peter Parish**)

Thomas Tighe (son):

Residence - Montpelier Hill, St. Paul Parish - September 2, 1852

No. 41 Deuzille Street - July 25, 1853

December 24, 1854

2 Hamilton Row - February 15, 1857

February 12, 1860

June 1, 1862

Occupation - Carpenter - September 2, 1852

July 25, 1853

December 24, 1854

Hurst

Builder - February 15, 1857

June 1, 1862

Carpenter & Builder - February 12, 1860

Margaret Blevins, daughter of David Blevins (daughter-in-law):

Residence - 4 Lower Baggot Street - September 2, 1852

David Blevins (father):

Occupation - Farmer

Thomas Tighe (father):

Occupation - Farmer

Wedding Witnesses:

Richard Eustace

Signature:

- Thomas Tighe & Unknown
    - Anne Tighe & Thomas Joseph Flood – 22 Apr 1873 (Marriage, **St. James Parish (RC)**)
        - Elizabeth Flood – b. 24 Apr 1873, bapt. 29 Apr 1873 (Baptism, **St. James Parish (RC)**)
        - Lawrence Flood – b. 21 Aug 1877, bapt. 24 Aug 1877 (Baptism, **St. James Parish (RC)**)
        - James Flood – b. 16 Mar 1880, bapt. 24 Mar 1880 (Baptism, **St. James Parish (RC)**)

Anne Tighe (daughter):

Residence - Golden Bridge - April 22, 1873

Tighe Surname Ireland: 1600s to 1900s

Thomas Flood, son of Lawrence Flood (son-in-law):

Residence - Golden Bridge - April 22, 1873

April 29, 1873

August 24, 1877

March 24, 1880

- o Thomas Tighe & Elizabeth Reilly – 2 Nov 1875 (Marriage, **St. James Parish** (RC))
  - ▪ Richard Thomas Tighe – b. 19 May 1877, bapt. 24 May 1877 (Baptism, **St. James Parish** (RC))
  - ▪ Anne Elizabeth Tighe – b. 28 Apr 1879, bapt. 6 May 1879 (Baptism, **St. James Parish** (RC))
  - ▪ Thomas Joseph Tighe – b. 15 Aug 1881, bapt. 25 Aug 1881 (Baptism, **St. James Parish** (RC))

Thomas Tighe (son):

Residence - Inchicore - May 24, 1877

May 6, 1879

August 25, 1881

8 Golden Bridge - November 2, 1875

Elizabeth Reilly, daughter of Richard Reilly (daughter-in-law):

Residence - 3 Golden Bridge - November 2, 1875

Wedding Witnesses:

Patrick Tighe & Mary Anne Hart

o Patrick Tighe & Catherine Rooney – 18 Jul 1882 (Marriage, **St. James Parish** (RC))

Patrick Tighe (son):

Residence - Golden Bridge - July 18, 1882

Catherine Rooney, daughter of Thomas Rooney (daughter-in-law):

Residence - Richmond - July 18, 1882

• Thomas Tighe & Unknown

o Elizabeth Tighe & John Enright – 26 Jan 1875 (Marriage, **Tralee Parish**)

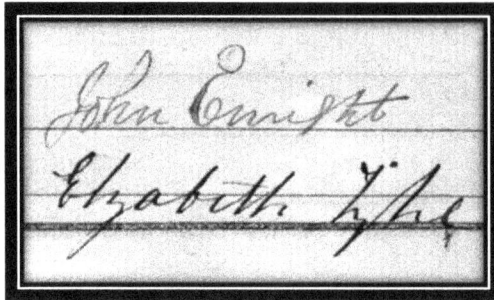

Signatures:

Elizabeth Tighe (daughter):

Residence - Oak Park, Tralee - January 26, 1875

Occupation - Servant - January 26, 1875

John Enright, son of John Enright (son-in-law):

Residence - Tralee Barracks - January 26, 1875

Occupation - Sergeant 8th Regiment - January 26, 1875

John Enright (father):

Occupation - Out Pensioner

Tighe Surname Ireland: 1600s to 1900s

Thomas Tighe (father):

   Occupation - Taylor

Wedding Witnesses:

William Kearins & Peter Bovenizer

Signatures:

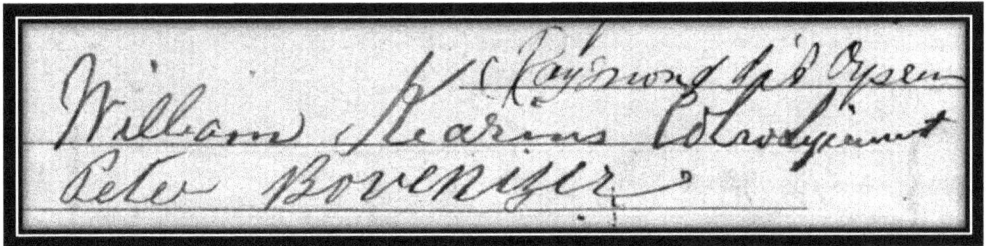

- Thomas Tighe & Unknown

  - Margaret Tighe & Timothy Reynolds – 24 Sep 1876 (Marriage, **St. Audoen Parish (RC)**)

    - Mary Reynolds – b. 29 Dec 1877, bapt. 11 Jan 1878 (Baptism, **St. Mary, Pro Cathedral Parish (RC)**)

Margaret Tighe (daughter):

   Residence - 16 Michael's Hill - September 24, 1876

Timothy Reynolds, son of Michael Reynolds (son-in-law):

   Residence - 6 West Essex Street - September 24, 1876

   41 Capel Street - January 11, 1878

Hurst

- Thomas John Tighe & Margaret Camilla Freke – 12 Dec 1838 (Marriage, **St. Mary Parish**)

Signatures:

Thomas John Tighe (husband):

    Residence - Drumgorland of Parsons Hill, Co. Down - December 12, 1838

Margaret Camilla Freke (wife):

    Residence - St. Mary Parish - December 12, 1838

Wedding Witnesses:

James Freke & William John Freke

Signatures:

- Thomas Mark Tighe & Unknown

  o Mary Tighe & Alexander Wallace – 31 Oct 1848 (Marriage, **St. Peter Parish**)

Signatures:

Mary Tighe (daughter):

   Residence - 4 Upper Pembroke Street, St. Peter Parish - October 31, 1848

Alexander Wallace, son of John Wallace (son-in-law):

   Residence - 22 Wentworth Place, St. Mark Parish - October 31, 1848

   Occupation - Sailor - October 31, 1848

   Relationship Status at Marriage - widow

John Wallace (father):

   Occupation - Gardener

Thomas Mark Tighe (father):

   Occupation - A Smith

Hurst

Wedding Witnesses:

Thomas Carroll & Dennis O'Keeffe

Signatures:

- Timothy Tighe & Catherine Sullivan

    o Catherine Tighe – bapt. 14 May 1835 (Baptism, **Drimoleague Parish** (RC))

    o Mary Tighe – bapt. 30 Jul 1836 (Baptism, **Bantry Parish** (RC))

- Timothy Tighe & Eleanor Burchill

    o John Tighe – bapt. 12 Feb 1843 (Baptism, **Drimoleague Parish** (RC))

- Timothy Tighe & Honor Unknown

    o James Tighe & Mary Elizabeth Slaney – 1 Oct 1873 (Marriage, **St. Andrew Parish** (RC))

James Tighe (son):

Residence - Waterford - October 1, 1873

Mary Elizabeth Slaney, daughter of William Slaney & Jane Unknown

(daughter-in-law):

Residence - Waterford - October 1, 1873

- Timothy Tighe & Judith McCarthy

  o John Tighe – bapt. 20 Feb 1843 (Baptism, **Drimoleague Parish (RC)**)

  o Ellen Tighe – bapt. 12 Jun 1848 (Baptism, **Drimoleague Parish (RC)**)

- Timothy Tighe & Rose Unknown

  o Christopher Tighe – bapt. 1772 (Baptism, **St. Andrew Parish (RC)**)

- Timothy Tighe & Unknown

  o Bridget Tighe – bapt. Oct 1781 (Baptism, **St. Michan Parish (RC)**)

- Unknown Tighe & Unknown

  o Alice Tighe

Signature:

- Unknown Tighe & Unknown

  o Dorothy Tighe

Signature:

- Unknown Tighe & Unknown

  o Dorothy Tighe

Signature:

- Unknown Tighe & Unknown

  o John Atkinson Tighe – b. 1811, bur. 5 Mar 1861 (Burial, **St. Catherine Parish**)

Signatures:

John Atkinson Tighe (son):

Residence - Dr. Stephen's Hospital - before March 5, 1861

Age at Death - 50 years

- Unknown Tighe & Unknown

  o Julia Tighe

Signature:

- Unknown Tighe & Unknown

  o St. Lawrence R. M. Tighe

Signatures:

- Unknown Tighe & Unknown

  o Thomas Tighe

Signature:

- Unknown Tighe & Unknown

  o Thomas Tighe

Signature:

- Unknown Tighe & Unknown

  o Thomas Tighe

Signature:

- Unknown Tighe & Unknown

  o Thomas Tighe

Signature:

- Unknown Tighe & Unknown

  o Unknown Tighe & Mary Gannon (1st Marriage)

  o Mary Gannon Tighe (2nd Marriage) & James Mellon – 2 May 1850

Signatures:

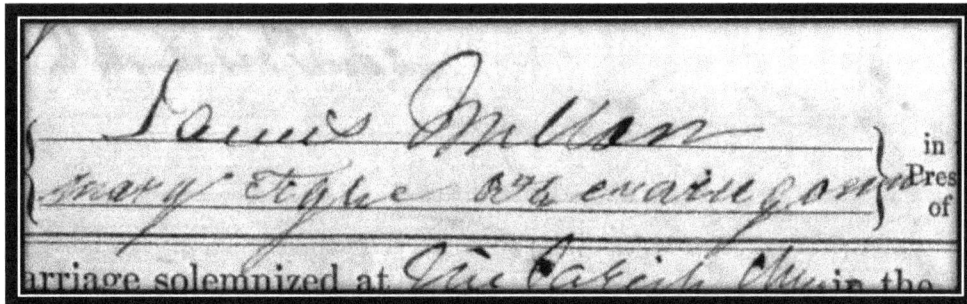

Mary Gannon Tighe, daughter of John Gannon & Unknown (daughter-in-law):

Residence - 21 Charlotte Street - May 2, 1850

Occupation - Milliner - May 2, 1850

Relationship Status at Marriage - widow

James Mellon, son of John Mellon (son-in-law):

Residence - 21 Charlotte Street - May 2, 1850

Occupation - Constable - May 2, 1850

John Mellon (father):

Occupation - Farmer

John Gannon (father):

Occupation - Servant

Hurst

Wedding Witnesses:

John Gannon & Anne Gannon

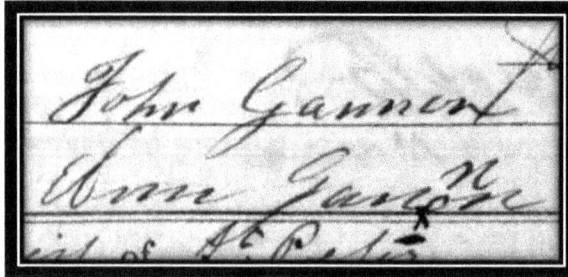

Signatures:

- Unknown Tighe & Unknown

  o W. Tighe

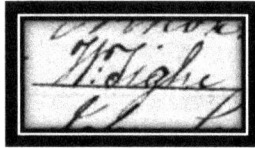

Signature:

W. Tighe (son):

Residence - 58 Henry Street - March 21, 1822

- Unknown Tighe & Unknown

  o William Tighe

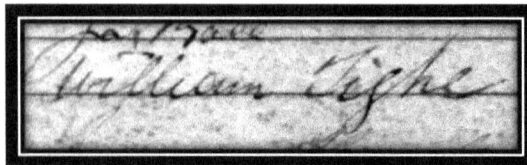

Signature:

- Unknown Tighe & Unknown

  o William Tighe

Signature:

- William Tighe & Anne Carroll, b. 1804, bur. 21 Oct 1838 (Burial, **St. Catherine Parish**) – 14 Apr 1823 (Marriage, **St. Mary Parish**)

Signatures:

  o Anne Susan Tighe – b. 29 Jul 1824, bapt. 4 Oct 1824 (Baptism, **St. Mary Parish**), bur. 5 Aug 1825 (Baptism, **St. Catherine Parish**)

Anne Tighe (daughter):

Residence - Capel Street - before August 5, 1825

Age at Death - 1 year

  o Frances Tighe – b. 26 May 1827, bapt. 4 Jul 1827 (Baptism, **St. Mary Parish**)

  o Anne Matilda Tighe – b. 1828, bapt. 6 Jul 1828 (Baptism, **St. Mary Parish**), bur. 27 Nov 1831 (Burial, **St. Catherine Parish**)

Hurst

Anne Matilda Tighe (daughter):

 Residence - Capel Street - before November 8, 1831

 Age at Death - 3 years

 Cause of Death - Scarletine (Scarlet Fever)

- Henry Bingham Tighe – bapt. 9 Jan 1831 (Baptism, **St. Mary Parish**)
- Clarissa Tighe – b. 1829, bapt. 14 Sep 1831 (Baptism, **St. Mary Parish**), bur. 9 Nov 1831 (Burial, **St. Catherine Parish**)

Clarissa Tighe (daughter):

 Residence - Capel Street - before November 9, 1831

 Age at Death - 2 years

 Cause of Death - Scarletine (Scarlet Fever)

- Anne Tighe – bapt. 11 Mar 1832 (Baptism, **St. Mary Parish**), bur. 21 Dec 1835 (Burial, **St. Catherine Parish**)

Anne Tighe (daughter):

 Residence - Capel Street - before December 21, 1835

 Age at Death - 3 ¾ years

 Cause of Death - Measles

- Mary Anne Tighe – bapt. 29 Jul 1833 (Baptism, **St. Mary Parish**)
- Matilda Susan Tighe – b. Feb 1835, bapt. 1 Feb 1835 (Baptism, **St. Mary Parish**), bur. 4 Nov 1835 (Burial, **St. Catherine Parish**)

Tighe Surname Ireland: 1600s to 1900s

Matilda Tighe (daughter):

Residence - Capel Street - before February 1, 1835

Age at Death - 9 Months

Cause of Death - Scarletine (Scarlet Fever)

- Marcella Elizabeth Tighe – bapt. 19 Jun 1836 (Baptism, **St. Mary Parish**)

- Emily Susan Tighe – b. 14 Mar 1838, bapt. 27 Apr 1838 (Baptism, **St. Mary Parish**)

William Tighe (father):

Residence - St. Mary Parish - April 14, 1823

Capel Street - October 4, 1824

July 4, 1827

July 29, 1833

120 Capel Street - July 6, 1828

January 9, 1831

September 14, 1831

March 11, 1832

February 1, 1835

June 19, 1836

April 27, 1838

Occupation - Apothecary - July 6, 1828

January 9, 1831

Hurst

September 14, 1831

March 11, 1832

February 1, 1835

June 19, 1836

April 27, 1838

Anne Carroll (mother):

Residence - St. Mary Parish - April 14, 1823

Capel Street - before October 21, 1838

Age at Death - 34 years

Cause of Death - fight in childbirth

Wedding Witnesses:

Henry Bingham & W. Unknown

Signatures:

- William Tighe & Catherine Curry
  - Mary Bridget Tighe & James Caffrey – 2 Oct 1881 (Marriage, St. Mary, Pro Cathedral Parish (RC))
    - Margaret Mary Caffrey – b. 21 Feb 1882, bapt. 3 Mar 1882 (Baptism, St. Mary, Pro Cathedral Parish (RC))

Tighe Surname Ireland: 1600s to 1900s

- William Patrick Joseph Caffrey – b. 13 Mar 1884, bapt. 21 Mar 1884 (Baptism, **St. Mary, Pro Cathedral Parish** (RC))

- James Patrick Caffrey – b. 12 Mar 1886, bapt. 12 Mar 1886 (Baptism, **St. Mary, Pro Cathedral Parish** (RC))

- James Caffrey – b. 25 Sep 1888, bapt. 5 Oct 1888 (Baptism, **St. Mary, Pro Cathedral Parish** (RC))

- Christopher Caffrey – b. 14 Dec 1889, bapt. 23 Dec 1889 (Baptism, **St. Mary, Pro Cathedral Parish** (RC))

- Charles Caffrey – b. 20 Jul 1891, bapt. 29 Jul 1891 (Baptism, **St. Mary, Pro Cathedral Parish** (RC))

- Elizabeth Mary Caffrey – b. 10 Sep 1891, bapt. 11 Sep 1891 (Baptism, **St. Mary, Pro Cathedral Parish** (RC))

- John Joseph Caffrey – b. 14 Jun 1894, bapt. 25 Jun 1894 (Baptism, **St. Mary, Pro Cathedral Parish** (RC))

- Elizabeth Caffrey – b. 6 Nov 1896, bapt. 16 Nov 1896 (Baptism, **St. Mary, Pro Cathedral Parish** (RC))

Mary Tighe (daughter):

Residence - 58 Amiens Street - October 2, 1881

James Caffrey, son of James Caffrey & Anne Reilly (son-in-law):

Residence - 11 Lower Liffey Street - October 5, 1888

6 King's Avenue - October 2, 1881

27 Gardiner's Lane - March 3, 1882

Hurst

21 Middle Abbey Street - December 23, 1889

Rotunda - July 29, 1891

7 Gardiner's Lane - March 21, 1884

March 12, 1886

September 11, 1891

41 Middle Abbey Street - June 25, 1894

November 16, 1896

- William Tighe & Catherine Gleeson
  - Margaret Tighe – bapt. 1839 (Baptism, St. Mary Parish (RC))
- William Tighe & Catherine Tighe
  - James Tighe – bapt. 4 Nov 1836 (Baptism, St. Mary, Pro Cathedral Parish (RC))
  - Mary Tighe – bapt. 18 Feb 1838 (Baptism, St. Mary, Pro Cathedral Parish (RC))
- William Tighe & Catherine Tighe
  - Teresa Tighe & John Smyth – 10 Oct 1860 (Marriage, St. Mary, Pro Cathedral Parish (RC))

Teresa Tighe (daughter):

Residence - 198 Great Britain Street - October 10, 1860

John Smyth, son of John Smyth & Mary Anne Unknown (son-in-law):

Residence - Woolwich - October 10, 1860

Wedding Witnesses:

James Tighe & Bridget Bower

Tighe Surname Ireland: 1600s to 1900s

- William Tighe & Catherine Unknown

  - Joshua Tighe – bapt. 2 Feb 1818 (Baptism, **St. Mary, Pro Cathedral Parish** (RC))

  - James Tighe – bapt. 10 Feb 1823 (Baptism, **St. Mary, Pro Cathedral Parish** (RC))

  - Edward Augustine Tighe – bapt. 11 Jul 1824 (Baptism, **St. Mary, Pro Cathedral Parish** (RC))

  - John Tighe – bapt. 14 May 1826 (Baptism, **St. Mary, Pro Cathedral Parish** (RC))

  - Mary Anne Tighe – bapt. 8 Sep 1830 (Baptism, **St. Mary, Pro Cathedral Parish** (RC))

  - Mary Anne Tighe – bapt. 8 Sep 1831 (Baptism, **St. Mary, Pro Cathedral Parish** (RC))

  - Thomas Tighe – bapt. 16 Sep 1834 (Baptism, **St. Mary, Pro Cathedral Parish** (RC))

William Tighe (father):

Residence - 20 Britain Street - February 2, 1818

- William Tighe & Catherine Unknown

  - Thomas Christopher Tighe – bapt. 7 Jan 1844 (Baptism, **St. Mary, Pro Cathedral Parish** (RC))

  - Catherine Mary Tighe – bapt. 6 Sep 1847 (Baptism, **St. Mary, Pro Cathedral Parish** (RC))

  - Mary Tighe – bapt. 28 Nov 1851 (Baptism, **St. Mary, Pro Cathedral Parish** (RC))

- William Tighe & Catherine Unknown

  - William Tighe – b. 1856, bapt. 1856 (Baptism, **St. Andrew Parish** (RC))

- William Tighe & Catherine Unknown

  - Patrick Tighe & Elizabeth Brophy – 17 Dec 1872 (Marriage, **St. Andrew Parish** (RC))

Hurst

Patrick Tighe (son):

Residence - 3 James Lane - December 17, 1872

Elizabeth Brophy, daughter of Fintan Brophy & Mary Unknown (daughter-in-law):

Residence - 3 James Lane - December 17, 1872

- William Tighe & Jane Unknown
  - William Henry Tighe – b. 8 Oct 1842, bapt. 23 Nov 1842 (Baptism, **St. Peter Parish**)
  - Frances Martha Tighe – b. 18 May 1844, bapt. 27 Jun 1844 (Baptism, **St. Peter Parish**)

William Tighe (father):

Residence - Ashbourne - November 23, 1842

Ratoath - June 27, 1844

Occupation - Clergyman - November 23, 1842

June 27, 1844

- William Tighe & Margaret Unknown
  - Teresa Tighe – bapt. 17 Nov 1833 (Baptism, **St. Mary, Pro Cathedral Parish** (RC))
- William Tighe & Mary Staines
  - Owen Tighe – b. 1896, bapt. 1896 (Baptism, **St. Andrew Parish** (RC))
  - Michael James Tighe – b. 1898, bapt. 1898 (Baptism, **St. Andrew Parish** (RC))
  - James Tighe – b. 1900, bapt. 1900 (Baptism, **St. Andrew Parish** (RC))
  - Edward Tighe – b. 1902, bapt. 1902 (Baptism, **St. Andrew Parish** (RC))

William Tighe (father):

Residence - 8 Stephen's Place - 1896

132

Tighe Surname Ireland: 1600s to 1900s

8 Hogan's Court - 1898

1900

3 James Lane - 1902

- William Tighe & Mary Unknown

    o Sterne (S t e r n e) Tighe – b. 26 May 1835, bapt. 21 Jun 1835 (Baptism, **Taney Parish**)

William Tighe (father):

Residence - Dundrum - June 21, 1835

- William Tighe & Teresa James

    o Francis Joseph Tighe – b. 1884, bapt. 1884 (Baptism, **St. Andrew Parish (RC)**)

    o William Tighe – b. 1888, bapt. 1888 (Baptism, **St. Andrew Parish (RC)**)

William Tighe (father):

Residence - 4 Trinity College - 1884

4 Cleothane Row - 1888

- William Tighe & Unknown

    o William Tighe – bapt. 23 May 1766 (Baptism, **St. Mary Parish**)

William Tighe (father):

Residence - Dominick Street - May 23, 1766

- William Frederick Fownes Tighe & Louisa Madeline Tighe

    o Charlotte Frances Tighe – b. 4 Jul 1826, bapt. 7 Aug 1826 (Baptism, **St. George Parish**)

Hurst

- William J. Tighe & Mary J. Hanlon

  - Henry Joseph Tighe – b. 22 Mar 1856, bapt. 2 Apr 1856 (Baptism, **St. Michan Parish** (RC))

William J. Tighe (father):

Residence - 9 Palmerston Place - April 2, 1856

Individual Baptisms/Births

- Esther Tighe – bapt. 29 Jan 1840 (Baptism, **St. Mary Parish**)

Esther Tighe (child):

Remarks about Birth - a foundling

- Sterne (S t e r n e) Tighe – bapt. Apr 1824 (Baptism, **St. Mark Parish**)

Sterne Tighe (child):

Residence - Erne Street - April 1824

Individual Burials

- A. Tighe – bur. 27 Jun 1837 (Burial, **St. George Parish**)

A. Tighe (deceased):

  Residence - Whitworth Hospital - before June 27, 1837

- Anne Tighe – bur. 15 Aug 1781 (Burial, **St. James Parish**)

Anne Tighe (deceased):

  Residence - Thomas Street - before August 15, 1781

- Anne Tighe – bur. 15 Jul 1811 (Burial, **St. James Parish**)

Anne Tighe (deceased):

  Residence - Fordham's Alley - before July 15, 1811

- Anne Tighe – bur. 21 May 1815 (Burial, **St. James Parish**)

Anne Tighe (deceased):

  Residence - Francis Street - before May 15, 1815

- Anne Tighe – bur. 29 Mar 1826 (Burial, **St. Luke Parish**)

Anne Tighe (deceased):

  Residence - New Market - before March 29, 1826

- Arthur Tighe – bur. 18 Mar 1802 (Burial, **St. Paul Parish**)

Tighe Surname Ireland: 1600s to 1900s

- Bridget Tighe – bur. 17 Jun 1801 (Burial, **St. James Parish**)

Bridget Tighe (deceased):

    Residence - Ardee Street - before June 17, 1801

- Catherine Tighe – bur. 20 Feb 1795 (Burial, **St. James Parish**)

Catherine Tighe (deceased):

    Residence - Thomas Street - before February 20, 1795

- Catherine Tighe – bur. 25 Feb 1795 (Burial, **St. Peter Parish**)

Catherine Tighe (deceased):

    Residence - Camden Street - before February 25, 1795

- Catherine Tighe – bur. 3 Jun 1799 (Burial, **St. James Parish**)

Catherine Tighe (deceased):

    Residence - Ardee Street - before June 3, 1799

- Catherine Tighe – bur. 7 Jun 1824 (Burial, **St. James Parish**)

Catherine Tighe (deceased):

    Residence - Essex Street - before June 7, 1824

- Christopher Tighe – bur. 31 Jul 1804 (Burial, **St. James Parish**)

Christopher Tighe (deceased):

    Residence - Coombe - before July 31, 1804

Hurst

- Christopher Tighe – bur. 25 Apr 1815 (Burial, **St. James Parish**)

Christopher Tighe (deceased):

   Residence - Cole Alley - before April **25, 1815**

- Clarinda Tighe – b. 1829, bur. 9 Nov 1831 (Burial, **St. Catherine Parish**)

Clarinda Tighe (deceased):

   Residence - Capel Street - before November 8, 1831

   Age at Death - **2 years**

- Daniel Tighe – bur. 9 Mar 1776 (Burial, **St. James Parish**)

Daniel Tighe (deceased):

   Residence - James Street - before March 9, 1776

- Duke Tighe – bur. 2 Jan 1737 (Burial, **St. Mary Parish**)
- E. Tighe – b. 1835, bur. 4 Dec 1837 (Burial, **St. George Parish**)

E. Tighe (deceased):

   Residence - Redmonds Court - before December 4, 1837

   Age at Death - **2 years**

- Edward Tighe – bur. 22 Sep 1808 (Burial, **St. Paul Parish**)
- Edward Tighe – bur. 23 Apr 1812 (Burial, **St. James Parish**)

Edward Tighe (deceased):

   Residence - Liffey Street - before April **23, 1812**

Tighe Surname Ireland: 1600s to 1900s

- Frances Tighe – bur. 20 Feb 1825 (Burial, **St. Paul Parish**)

- Francis Tighe – bur. 21 Nov 1673 (Burial, **St. Michan Parish**)

Francis Tighe (deceased):

Occupation - Soap Boiler - before November 21, 1673

- Francis Tighe – bur. 7 Dec 1807 (Burial, **St. James Parish**)

Francis Tighe (deceased):

Residence - New Market - before December 7, 1807

- Francis Tighe – bur. 30 Sep 1824 (Burial, **St. James Parish**)

Francis Tighe (deceased):

Residence - Lower Liffey Street - before September 30, 1824

- George Tighe – bur. 24 Sep 1783 (Burial, **St. Mark Parish**)

- Jane Tighe (child) – bur. 21 Sep 1742 (Burial, **St. Paul Parish**)

- Jane Tighe – bur. 27 Mar 1804 (Burial, **St. Mary Parish**)

Jane Tighe (deceased):

Residence - Willis Town - before March 27, 1804

- Joan Tighe – bur. 25 Mar 1735 (Burial, **St. Mary Parish**)

- John Tighe – bur. 21 Oct 1726 (Burial, **St. Mary Parish**)

- John Tighe – bur. 17 Oct 1783 (Burial, **St. Paul Parish**)

Hurst

- John Tighe – b. Feb 1830, bur. 13 Jul 1830 (Burial, **St. Mark Parish**)

John Tighe (deceased):

Residence - Shaw Street - before July 13, 1830

Age at Death - 6 months

- John Tighe – b. 1826, d. 31 Jul 1856, bur. 1 Aug 1856 (Burial, **Arbour Hill Barracks Parish**)

John Tighe (deceased):

Occupation - Private 38th Regiment - July 31, 1856

Age at Death - 30 years

- John F. Tighe – b. Aug 1856, bur. 3 Sep 1856 (Burial, **St. George Parish**)

John F. Tighe (deceased):

Residence - Summer Hill - before September 3, 1856

Age at Death - 6 weeks

- Joseph Tighe – b. 1826, bur. 13 Dec 1828 (Burial, **St. Mark Parish**)

Joseph Tighe (deceased):

Residence - Townsend Street - before December 13, 1828

Age at Death - 2 years

- Judith Tighe – bur. 12 Feb 1794 (Burial, **Glasnevin Parish**)

Judith Tighe (deceased):

Residence - Britain Street - before February 12, 1794

Tighe Surname Ireland: 1600s to 1900s

- Julie Tighe – b. Aug 1863, bur. 14 May 1864 (Burial, **St. George Parish**)

Julie Tighe (deceased):

Residence - 6 Johnston's Court - before May 14, 1864

Age at Death - 10 months

- Lawrence Tighe – bur. 2 Feb 1799 (Burial, **St. James Parish**)

Lawrence Tighe (deceased):

Residence - Cork Street - before February 2, 1799

- Lucy Tighe – bur. 18 Aug 1811 (Burial, **St. James Parish**)

Lucy Tighe (deceased):

Residence - James Street - before August 18, 1811

- Margaret Tighe – b. 1815, d. 12 Dec 1880, bur. 1880 (Burial, **Clondalkin Parish**)

Margaret Tighe (deceased):

Residence - Clondalkin - December 12, 1880

Age at Death - 65 years

- Mary Tighe – bur. 9 Jan 1768 (Burial, **St. Paul Parish**)

Mary Tighe (deceased):

Residence - King Street - before January 9, 1768

- Mary Tighe – bur. 23 Dec 1780 (Burial, **St. James Parish**)

Mary Tighe (deceased):

Hurst

Residence - B -- Lane - before December 23, 1780

- Mary Tighe – bur. 12 Aug 1789 (Burial, **St. Paul Parish**)

- Mary Tighe (infant) – bur. 17 Sep 1811 (Burial, **St. Mark Parish**)

Mary Tighe (infant) (deceased):

Residence - Westmoreland Street - before September 17, 1811

- Mary Tighe – b. 1788, d. 30 Jun 1868, bur. 1868 (Burial, **St. James Parish**)

Mary Tighe (deceased):

Residence - South Dublin Union - June 30, 1868

Age at Death - 80 years

- Mary Anne Tighe – bur. 13 Apr 1824 (Burial, **St. Werburgh Parish**)

Mary Anne Tighe (deceased):

Residence - 42 Castle Street - before April 13, 1824

- Matilda C. Tighe – b. Oct 1824, bur. 8 Nov 1825 (Burial, **St. Catherine Parish**)

Matilda C. Tighe (deceased):

Residence - Capel Street - before November 8, 1825

Age at Death - 11 months

- Matthew Tighe – d. 2 May 1832, bur. 1832 (Burial, **Clondalkin Parish**)

Matthew Tighe (deceased):

Residence - 9ᵗʰ Lock - May 2, 1832

Tighe Surname Ireland: 1600s to 1900s

- Matthew Tighe – b. 1815, d. 4 Nov 1875, bur. 1875 (Burial, **Clondalkin Parish**)

Matthew Tighe (deceased):

Residence - Moorfield, Clondalkin - November 4, 1875

Age at Death - 60 years

- Michael Tighe – bur. 26 Nov 1817 (Burial, **St. James Parish**)

Michael Tighe (deceased):

Residence - James Gate - before November 26, 1817

- Nicholas Tighe – bur. 16 Aug 1776 (Burial, **St. James Parish**)

Nicholas Tighe (deceased):

Residence - Ranford Street - before August 16, 1776

- Patrick Tighe – bur. 8 Feb 1720 (Burial, **St. Catherine Parish**)
- Patrick Tighe – bur. 6 Apr 1781 (Burial, **St. James Parish**)

Patrick Tighe (deceased):

Residence - Dolphin's Barn - before April 6, 1781

- Patrick Tighe – b. 1802, bur. 5 Apr 1883 (Burial, **Taney Parish**)

Patrick Tighe (deceased):

Residence - Asylum - before April 5, 1883

Age at Death - 81 years

- Peter Tighe – bur. 3 Sep 1809 (Burial, **St. Paul Parish**)

Hurst

- Peter Tighe – d. 21 May 1827, bur. 1827 (Burial, **Clondalkin Parish**)

Peter Tighe (deceased):

  Residence - 9th Lock - May 21, 1827

- Richard Tighe – bur. 15 Jan 1753 (Burial, **St. Paul Parish**)

Richard Tighe (deceased):

  Occupation - Esquire - before January 15, 1753

- Richard Tighe – bur. 9 Feb 1812 (Burial, **St. Paul Parish**)

- Robert Tighe – bur. 28 Sep 1780 (Burial, **St. Paul Parish**)

- Robert Tighe – bur. 2 Feb 1828 (Burial, **Clontarf Parish**)

Robert Tighe (deceased):

  Residence - City of Dublin - before February 2, 1828

  Occupation - Major

- Sarah Tighe – bur. 9 Jan 1773 (Burial, **St. Audoen Parish**)

- Susan Tighe – b. 1770, d. 24 Jan 1814, bur, 1814 (Burial, **St. Peter Parish**)

Susanna Tighe (deceased):

  Age at Death - 44 years

- Thomas Tighe – bur. 30 Mar 1795 (Burial, **St. James Parish**)

Thomas Tighe (deceased):

  Residence - Dirty Lane - before March 30, 1795

Tighe Surname Ireland: 1600s to 1900s

- Thomas Tighe – bur. 3 Nov 1808 (Burial, **St. Peter Parish**)

Thomas Tighe (deceased):

Residence - Camden Street - before November 3, 1808

- Unknown Tighe – bur. 18 Sep 1756 (Burial, **St. Nicholas Without Parish**)

Unknown Tighe (deceased):

Residence - Co. Kildare - before September 18, 1756

- Unknown Tighe (Mr.) – b. 1768, bur. 22 Apr 1779 (Burial, **St. Nicholas Without Parish**)

Unknown Tighe (Mr.) (deceased):

Residence - Market - before April 22, 1779

Age at Death - 11 years

- Unknown Tighe (Mrs.) – b. 1768, bur. 13 Jun 1779 (Burial, **St. Nicholas Without Parish**)

Unknown Tighe (Mrs.) (deceased):

Residence - Francis Street - before June 13, 1779

Age at Death - 11 years

- Unknown Tighe – bur. 29 Apr 1790 (Burial, **St. Nicholas Without Parish**)

Unknown Tighe (deceased):

Residence - New Street - before April 29, 1790

Hurst

- Unknown Tighe – b. Jul 1831, bur. 6 Aug 1831 (Burial, **St. Catherine Parish**)

Unknown Tighe (deceased):

    Residence - Capel Street - before August 6, 1831

    Age at Death - 1 month

- William Tighe – b. 1800, bur. 6 Feb 1848 (Burial, **St. Catherine Parish**)

William Tighe (deceased):

    Residence - Capel Street - before February 6, 1848

    Age at Death - 48 years

- William Tighe – b. 1799, bur. 28 Jan 1879 (Burial, **Taney Parish**)

William Tighe (deceased):

    Residence - Rosemount Dundrum, Co. Dublin - before January 28, 1879

    Age at Death - 80 years

Individual Marriages

- Agnes Mary Tighe & Christopher Joseph Byrne (B y r n e)

  o Catherine Agnes Byrne (B y r n e) – b. 21 Jan 1904, bapt. 24 Jan 1904 (Baptism, St. Joseph Parish (RC))

Christopher Joseph Byrne (father):

Residence - Terenure House, Terenure - January 24, 1904

- Anne Tighe & Christopher Walsh

  o Mary Frances Walsh – b. 9 Jan 1891, bapt. 14 Jan 1891 (Baptism, St. Mary, Pro Cathedral Parish (RC))

  o Margaret Mary Walsh – b. 28 May 1892, bapt. 3 Jun 1892 (Baptism, St. Mary, Pro Cathedral Parish (RC))

  o Anne Josephine Walsh – b. 25 Aug 1893, bapt. 1 Sep 1893 (Baptism, St. Mary, Pro Cathedral Parish (RC))

  o Catherine Mary Margaret Walsh – b. 20 Jul 1896, bapt. 24 Jul 1896 (Baptism, St. Mary, Pro Cathedral Parish (RC))

  o Elizabeth Mary Walsh – b. 2 May 1898, bapt. 16 May 1898 (Baptism, St. Mary, Pro Cathedral Parish (RC))

  o Mary Jane Frances Walsh – b. 1 Aug 1900, bapt. 10 Aug 1900 (Baptism, St. Mary, Pro Cathedral Parish (RC))

Hurst

Christopher Walsh (father):

Residence - 1 Cole's Lane - January 14, 1891

June 3, 1892

September 1, 1893

4 Cole's Lane - July 24, 1896

3 Lower Dominick Street - May 16, 1898

August 10, 1900

- Anne Tighe & James Blythe – 24 Jun 1844 (Marriage, **St. Peter Parish**)
  - Sarah Mary Anne Blythe – bapt. 29 Mar 1848 (Baptism, **St. Nicholas Parish** (RC))
  - John Blythe – bapt. 16 Apr 1849 (Baptism, **St. Nicholas Parish** (RC))

Anne Tighe (mother):

Residence - **25** Bishop Street - June 24, 1844

James Blythe (father):

Residence - Beggar's Bush Barracks - June 24, 1844

- Anne Tighe & James Hugh
  - James Hugh – bapt. 14 Jun 1850 (Baptism, **St. Nicholas Parish** (RC))
- Anne Tighe & John Casey – 14 Feb 1805 (Marriage, **St. Andrew Parish** (RC))
- Anne Tighe & John Connor
  - Catherine Connor & John Bracken – 26 Oct 1856 (Marriage, **St. Nicholas Parish** (RC))

Tighe Surname Ireland: 1600s to 1900s

Catherine Connor (daughter):

Residence - 18 Charlotte Street - October 26, 1856

John Bracken, son of Patrick Bracken & Mary Duggan (son-in-law):

Residence - 5 Beresford Street - October 26, 1856

Wedding Witnesses:

John Connor & Margaret Dolan

- Anne Tighe & Mathias Keenan – 1 Nov 1840 (Marriage, **St. Andrew Parish (RC)**)

- Anne Tighe & Michael Byrne (B y r n e) – 16 Jan 1856 (Marriage, **St. Andrew Parish (RC)**)

- Anne Tighe & Patrick Bourke – 28 Feb 1797 (Marriage, **St. Andrew Parish (RC)**)

- Anne Tighe & Gulielmo William Martin

  o Sarah Christine Martin – b. 1872, bapt. 1873 (Baptism, **St. Andrew Parish (RC)**)

  o Joseph Martin – b. 11 Mar 1875, bapt. 25 May 1875 (Baptism, **St. Audoen Parish (RC)**)

William Martin (father):

Residence - 7 Bedford Row - 1872

O'Keefe Cottage, Kennedy's Lane - May 25, 1875

- Anne Tighe & Michael Fylan

  o Michael Fylan – bapt. Dec 1830 (Baptism, **St. Catherine Parish (RC)**)

- Barbara Tighe & Michael Sandys – 22 Jul 1776 (Marriage, **St. Anne Parish**)

Michael Sandys, son of Michael Sandys (husband):

Occupation - Reverend - July 22, 1776

- Bridget Tighe & John Prendergast – 9 Jun 1850 (Marriage, **St. Mary, Pro Cathedral Parish (RC)**)

- Bridget Tighe & Joseph O'Connell

  - Daniel O'Connell – bapt. 24 Jul 1843 (Baptism, **St. Mary, Pro Cathedral Parish (RC)**)

- Bridget Tighe & Michael O'Maily

  - Christopher James O'Maily – b. 31 Dec 1865, bapt. 1 Jan 1866 (Baptism, **St. Michan Parish (RC)**)

  - Mary O'Maily – b. 11 Aug 1870, bapt. 12 Aug 1870 (Baptism, **St. Michan Parish (RC)**)

Michael O'Maily (father):

Residence - 27 Greek Street - January 1, 1866

August 12, 1870

- Bridget Tighe & Michael O'Reilly

  - Margaret O'Reilly – b. 1867, bapt. 1867 (Baptism, **St. Andrew Parish (RC)**)

  - Mary Bridget O'Reilly – b. 1869, bapt. 1869 (Baptism, **St. Andrew Parish (RC)**)

  - Christine O'Reilly – b. 24 Jul 1872, bapt. 30 Jul 1872 (Baptism, **St. James Parish (RC)**)

  - Anne O'Reilly – b. 22 Jan 1874, bapt. 27 Jan 1874 (Baptism, **St. James Parish (RC)**)

Michael O'Reilly (father):

Residence - 31 King Street - 1867

31 South King Street - 1869

High Road, Kilmainham - July 30, 1872

4 High Road, Kilmainham - January 27, 1874

Tighe Surname Ireland: 1600s to 1900s

- Bridget Tighe & Robert Parker

  o Harriet Alice Parker – b. 31 Sep 1861, bapt. 18 Oct 1861 (Baptism, **St. James Parish** (RC))

Robert Parker (father):

Residence - Dolphin's Barn - October 18, 1861

- Bridget Tighe & Thomas O'Healy

  o Margaret O'Healy – b. 5 Jun 1833, bapt. 5 Jun 1833 (Baptism, **Tralee Parish** (RC))

Thomas O'Healy (father):

Residence - Tralee - June 5, 1833

- Bridget Tighe & Thomas Wallace

  o David Wallace – b. 8 Dec 1831, bapt. 8 Dec 1831 (Baptism, **Tralee Parish** (RC))

Thomas Wallace (father):

Residence - Tralee - December 8, 1831

- Catherine Tighe & Bartholomew Caffrey – 16 Jan 1832 (Marriage, **St. Andrew Parish** (RC))
- Catherine Tighe & Edward Kelly – 30 Sep 1816 (Marriage, **Lucan Parish** (RC)) (Marriage, **St. Mary, Haddington Road Parish** (RC))

  o Michael Kelly – bapt. 12 Jun 1818 (Baptism, **St. Catherine Parish** (RC))

Wedding Witnesses:

Hugh Tighe, Anthony Saurin, Elizabeth Tighe, & Jane Pheir

Hurst

- Catherine Tighe & Edward Ramsey

  o Susan Ramsey – b. 19 Jan 1880, bapt. 9 Feb 1880 (Baptism, **St. Mary, Pro Cathedral Parish** (RC))

Edward Ramsey (father):

Residence - 60 Marlboro Street - February 9, 1880

- Catherine Tighe & Henry Finn

  o Daniel Finn – bapt. Dec 1791 (Baptism, **St. Catherine Parish** (RC))

  o Henry Finn – bapt. 29 Oct 1801 (Baptism, **St. Nicholas Parish** (RC))

- Catherine Tighe & John McDermott (M c D e r m o t t) – 23 Jun 1851 (Marriage, **St. Andrew Parish** (RC))

- Catherine Tighe & John McNeill

  o John James McNeill – b. 17 Jun 1877, bapt. 20 Jun 1877 (Baptism, **St. Lawrence Parish** (RC))

John McNeill (father):

Residence - 4[Hard to Read] **Lynch Place - June 20, 1877**

- Catherine Tighe & Martin Sweeny – 6 Feb 1837 (Marriage, **Rathfarnham Parish** (RC))

  o Elizabeth Sweeny – bapt. 16 Jul 1843 (Baptism, **St. Catherine Parish** (RC))

  o Elizabeth Sweeny – bapt. 16 Nov 1845 (Baptism, **St. Catherine Parish** (RC))

  o Bridget Sweeny – bapt. 26 Jan 1849 (Baptism, **St. Catherine Parish** (RC))

Tighe Surname Ireland: 1600s to 1900s

- Catherine Tighe & Robert Cunningham – 23 Jan 1821 (Marriage, **St. Audoen Parish** (RC))

  o Bridget Cunningham – bapt. 17 Apr 1833 (Baptism, **St. Nicholas Parish** (RC))

Wedding Witnesses:

Bryan Cunningham & Jane Monks

- Catherine Tighe & Thomas Coughlan – Unclear (Marriage, **St. Peter Parish**)

Catherine Tighe (wife):

   Residence - Portabello Canal Place

Thomas Coughlan (husband):

   Residence - Portabello Canal Place

- Catherine Tighe & William H. W. Newenham – 25 Jul 1807 (Marriage, **St. Andrew Parish**)

- Cecelia Tighe & Joseph Garland – 6 Jan 1851 (Marriage, **St. Andrew Parish** (RC))

  o Patrick Garland – b. 1862, bapt. 1862 (Baptism, **St. Andrew Parish** (RC))

Joseph Garland (father):

   Residence - No. 3 Lee's Lane - 1862

- Christine Tighe & Michael Traynor

  o Catherine Traynor – bapt. 29 Jul 1828 (Baptism, **St. Nicholas Parish** (RC))

- Clare Tighe & David Unknown – 26 Nov 1841 (Marriage, **St. Andrew Parish** (RC))

- Cordelia Tighe & James Horish – 14 Sep 1751 (Marriage, **St. Paul Parish**)

James Horish (husband):

   Occupation - Esquire - September 14, 1751

- Dorothy Tighe & Robert Mowland – 19 Dec 1741 (Marriage, **St. Paul Parish**)

Robert Mowland (husband):

    Occupation - Esquire - December 19, 1741

- Eleanor Tighe & John Power – 29 Jul 1851 (Marriage, **St. Nicholas Parish (RC)**)

- Elizabeth Tighe & Bernard (B e r n a r d) McManiele

    o   James McManiele – bapt. 1844 (Baptism, **Sandyford Parish (RC)**)

- Elizabeth Tighe & David McConnell – 22 Jan 1844 (Marriage, **St. Mary Parish (RC)**)

    o   Catherine McConnell – bapt. 1847 (Baptism, **St. Mary Parish (RC)**)

    o   Margaret McConnell – bapt. 1849 (Baptism, **St. Mary Parish (RC)**)

- Elizabeth Tighe & Frank Sheridan

    o   Anne Sheridan – bapt. 17 Jul 1829 (Baptism, **St. Catherine Parish (RC)**)

- Elizabeth Tighe & George Anderson – 7 Aug 1833 (Marriage, **St. George Parish**)

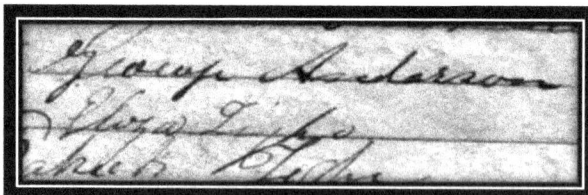

Signatures:

Elizabeth Tighe (wife):

    Residence - St. George Parish - August 7, 1833

George Anderson (husband):

    Residence - Rutland Square North, St. Mary's Parish - August 7, 1833

Wedding Witnesses:

Patrick Tighe, William Flood, & James Edmiston

Signatures:

- Elizabeth Tighe & George Coyle – 17 Dec 1791 (Marriage, **St. Catherine Parish (RC)**)

Wedding Witnesses:

Michael Tighe, Elizabeth Unknown, John Reilly, & Richard Mangan

- Elizabeth Tighe & Henry Free – 1 Jun 1829 (Marriage, **St. George Parish**)

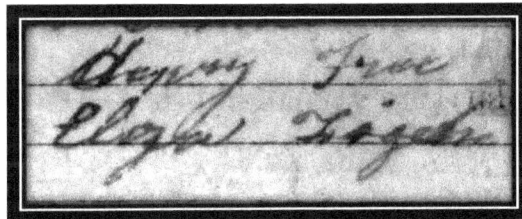

Signatures:

Elizabeth Tighe (wife):

> **Residence - St. George Parish - June 1, 1829**

Henry Free (husband):

> **Residence - St. George Parish - June 1, 1829**

Hurst

Wedding Witnesses:

John Hare & Benjamin Ray

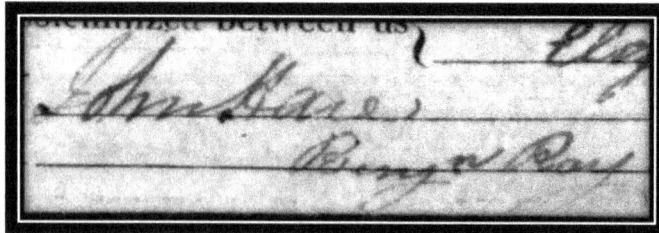

Signatures:

- Elizabeth Tighe & James Kavanagh – 4 Aug 1819 (Marriage, **St. Audoen Parish** (RC))

    o Bridget Kavanagh – bapt. 1823 (Baptism, **St. Nicholas Parish** (RC))

    o Elizabeth Kavanagh – bapt. 23 Jan 1825 (Baptism, **Rathmines Parish** (RC))

    o Sarah Kavanagh – bapt. Oct 1826 (Baptism, **Rathmines Parish** (RC))

    o Charles Kavanagh – bapt. 6 Jul 1828 (Baptism, **Rathmines Parish** (RC))

    o Christopher Kavanagh – bapt. 15 Sep 1831 (Baptism, **Rathmines Parish** (RC))

    o Sarah Kavanagh – bapt. Jun 1833 (Baptism, **Rathmines Parish** (RC))

    o Charles Kavanagh – bapt. 30 Nov 1834 (Baptism, **Rathmines Parish** (RC))

    o John Kavanagh – bapt. 2 Apr 1837 (Baptism, **Rathmines Parish** (RC))

Wedding Witnesses:

Thomas Mullen & Esther Tighe

- Elizabeth Tighe & James Kenny – 11 Oct 1865 (Marriage, **St. Mary Parish** (RC))

    o Andrew Kenny – bapt. 1865 (Baptism, **St. Mary Parish** (RC))

    o James Kenny – b. 1868, bapt. 1868 (Baptism, **St. Mary Parish** (RC))

    o Bridget Kenny – b. 1870, bapt. 1870 (Baptism, **St. Mary Parish** (RC))

    o Catherine Kenny – b. 1872, bapt. 1872 (Baptism, **St. Mary Parish** (RC))

- o Daniel Kenny – b. 1874, bapt. 1874 (Baptism, **St. Mary Parish** (RC))

- o Michael Kenny – b. 1876, bapt. 1876 (Baptism, **St. Mary Parish** (RC))

- o Patrick Kenny – b. 2 Nov 1877, bapt. 5 Nov 1877 (Baptism, **St. Mary, Haddington Road Parish** (RC))

- o Elizabeth Mary Kenny – b. 6 Aug 1879, bapt. 11 Aug 1879 (Baptism, **St. Mary, Haddington Road Parish** (RC))

- o Michael Kenny – b. 1882, bapt. 1882 (Baptism, **St. Andrew Parish** (RC))

James Kenny (father):

Residence - 10 Flemings Lane - November 5, 1877

        6 Flemings Place - August 11, 1879

        4 Leeson Place - 1882

- Elizabeth Tighe & Patrick Duffy – 24 Jan 1832 (Marriage, **St. Nicholas Parish** (RC))
- Elizabeth Tighe & Patrick Gahan – 15 Aug 1819 (Marriage, **St. Mary, Pro Cathedral Parish** (RC))

Wedding Witnesses:

Francis Tighe & Mary Tighe

- Elizabeth Tighe & Richard Pollard
  - o Christopher Pollard – bapt. 2 Jan 1834 (Baptism, **St. Michan Parish** (RC))
  - o Mary Anne Pollard – bapt. 11 Nov 1837 (Baptism, **St. Michan Parish** (RC))
- Elizabeth Tighe & Thomas Donnelly
  - o Edward P. G. Donnelly – b. 12 Dec 1871, bapt. 17 Dec 1871 (Baptism, **Rathmines Parish** (RC))

- o Mary Margaret Donnelly, b. 3 Nov 1873, bapt. 4 Nov 1873 (Baptism, **Rathmines Parish (RC)**) & Frederick E. Davis – 27 Jun 1895 (Marriage, **Harrington Street Parish** (RC))

Mary Margaret Donnelly (daughter):

Residence - 21 Harrington Street - June 27, 1895

Frederick E. Davis, son of Frederick Davis & Emily Bacholer (son-in-law):

Residence - St. Margaret Murrions - June 27, 1895

Thomas Donnelly (father):

Residence-Harrington Street - December 17, 1871

November 4, 1873

- Ellen Tighe & Edward Dalton
  - o Margaret Dalton & William Murrin – 22 Apr 1883 (Marriage, **St. Mary, Pro Cathedral Parish** (RC))

Margaret Dalton (daughter):

Residence - 70 Upper Dorset Street - April 22, 1883

William Murrin, son of William Murrin & Catherine Fox (son-in-law):

Residence - 70 Upper Dorset Street - April 22, 1883

- Ellen Tighe & James Carroll – 23 Oct 1825 (Marriage, **Lucan Parish** (RC))
  - o James Carroll – bapt. 1826 (Baptism, **Lucan Parish** (RC))
- Ellen Tighe & John Power
  - o Anne Power – bapt. 12 May 1849 (Baptism, **St. Catherine Parish** (RC))
  - o Anne Power – bapt. 17 Jan 1851 (Baptism, **St. Catherine Parish** (RC))

Tighe Surname Ireland: 1600s to 1900s

- Ellen Tighe & Peter Tool

  o Jane Tool – bapt. 13 Apr 1835 (Baptism, **St. James Parish (RC)**)

- Ellen Tighe & Richard McEvoy

  o Mary Anne McEvoy & James Finn – 1 Oct 1890 (Marriage, **St. Mary, Pro Cathedral Parish (RC)**)

Mary Anne McEvoy (daughter):

Residence - 1 Lower Dominick Street - October 1, 1890

James Finn, son of Dennis Finn & Mary Cogan (son-in-law):

Residence - 1 Lower Dominick Street - October 1, 1890

- Ellen Frances Tighe & Joseph Patrick Tighe Dennis

  o James Reynolds Tighe Dennis – b. 1902, bapt. 1902 (Baptism, **St. Andrew Parish (RC)**)

Joseph Patrick Tighe Dennis (father):

Residence - 122 Lower Baggot Street - 1902

- Frances Tighe & William Cructhley – 12 Feb 1683 (Marriage, **St. Michan Parish**)

William Crutchley (husband):

Occupation - Joiner - February 12, 1683

- Honor Tighe & Dennis McCarthy

  o Patrick McCarthy – bapt. 2 Jul 1844 (Baptism, **Drimoleague Parish (RC)**)

- Honor Tighe & Patrick Regan – 21 Feb 1862 (Marriage, **Clonakilty Parish (RC)**)

- Isabel Tighe & Patrick McCabe – 21 Sep 1829 (Marriage, **St. Michan Parish (RC)**)

  o John McCabe – bapt. 15 Aug 1830 (Baptism, **SS. Michael & John Parish (RC)**)

Hurst

- Jane Tighe & Francis Edmond

  - John Edmond – bapt. 21 Jun 1785 (Baptism, **St. Catherine Parish** (RC))

- Jane Tighe & Joshua Nunn – 10 Apr 1753 (Marriage, **St. Audoen Parish**)

Joshua Nunn (husband):

Occupation - Esquire - April 10, 1753

- Jane Tighe & Patrick Donovan

  - Anne Donovan – b. 4 Aug 1876, bapt. 8 Aug 1876 (Baptism, **St. James Parish** (RC))

Patrick Donovan (father):

Residence - 9 Crumlin Road - August 8, 1876

- Jane Tighe & Thomas Duffy

  - Catherine Duffy – bapt. 26 Oct 1836 (Baptism, **St. Nicholas Parish** (RC))

- Joan Tighe & John Fitzsimons

  - Anne Fitzsimons – b. 11 Jul 1878, bapt. Jul 1878 (Baptism, **St. Catherine Parish** (RC))

John Fitzsimons (father):

Residence - 13 Pimlico - July 1878

- Julie Tighe & Maurice Doyle – 2 Feb 1862 (Marriage, **St. Mary Parish** (RC))

- Julie Tighe & Robert Malone

  - Charlotte Malone – bapt. 27 Apr 1863 (Baptism, **St. Mary, Pro Cathedral Parish** (RC))

Robert Malone (father):

Residence - 14 Moore Street - April 27, 1863

Tighe Surname Ireland: 1600s to 1900s

- Julie Tighe & John Maloney

  o Honor Maloney – b. 20 Sep 1863, bapt. 5 Oct 1863 (Baptism, **St. Mary, Pro Cathedral Parish (RC)**)

  o John J. Maloney – b. Mar 1866, bapt. 5 Jul 1871 (Baptism, **St. Mary, Pro Cathedral Parish (RC)**)

John Mullowney (father):

Residence - 14 Moore Street - October 5, 1863

Upper Rutland Street - July 5, 1871

- M. Anne Tighe & Thomas Everatt – 8 Sep 1811 (Marriage, **St. Mary, Pro Cathedral Parish (RC)**)

- Mable Tighe & James Wilson – 2 Sep 1751 (Marriage, **St. Paul Parish**)

James Wilson (husband):

Occupation - Esquire - September 2, 1751

- Margaret Tighe & Bernard (B e r n a r d) Plunkett

  o Eleanor Plunkett & Christopher Mahon – 9 Feb 1869 (Marriage, **Ruthmines Parish (RC)**)

Eleanor Plunkett (daughter):

Residence - Belgrave Square - February 9, 1869

Christopher Mahon, son of John Mahon & Bridget Cowley (son-in-law):

Residence - Church Lane - February 9, 1869

Hurst

- Margaret Tighe & Daniel Callahan

  o William Callahan – b. 12 Jun 1877, bapt. 15 Jun 1877 (Baptism, **St. Lawrence Parish (RC)**)

Daniel Callahan (father):

Residence - 28 Coburgh Place - June 15, 1877

- Margaret Tighe & Dennis Healy – 3 Feb 1815 (Baptism, **Lixnaw Parish (RC)**)

Margaret Tighe (wife):

Residence - Rathie - February 3, 1815

- Margaret Tighe & Gulielmo Byrne (B y r n e)

  o Peter Byrne (B y r n e) & Bridget Kearney (K e a r n e y) – 27 Sep 1874 (Marriage, **Rathmines Parish (RC)**)

Peter Byrne (son):

Residence - Harold's Cross - September 27, 1874

Bridget Kearney, daughter of Michael Kearney & Anne Devlin (daughter-in-law):

Residence - Greenmount - September 27, 1874

- Margaret Tighe & John Byrne (B y r n e) – 5 Jan 1830 (Marriage, **St. Andrew Parish (RC)**)

- Margaret Tighe & John Conway – 8 Feb 1850 (Marriage, **St. Nicholas Parish (RC)**)

- Margaret Tighe & John Verlin

  o Julie Verlin – b. 17 Jan 1875, bapt. 21 Jan 1875 (Baptism, **St. James Parish (RC)**)

  o Mary Bridget Verlin – b. 1 Feb 1877, bapt. 5 Feb 1877 (Baptism, **St. Mary, Pro Cathedral Parish (RC)**)

- John Verlin – b. 27 Oct 1878, bapt. 30 Oct 1878 (Baptism, **St. Mary, Pro Cathedral Parish (RC)**)

- Margaret Verlin – b. 7 Oct 1880, bapt. 11 Oct 1880 (Baptism, **St. Mary, Pro Cathedral Parish (RC)**)

- Bridget Verlin – b. 30 Jan 1882, bapt. 3 Feb 1882 (Baptism, **St. Mary, Pro Cathedral Parish (RC)**)

John Verlin (father):

Residence - No. 12 New Kilmainham - January 21, 1875

34 Mabbot Street - February 5, 1877

1 Upper Dorset Street - October 30, 1878

October 11, 1880

February 3, 1882

- Margaret Tighe & Lewis Moore – 15 Sep 1801 (Marriage, **St. Catherine Parish (RC)**)

Wedding Witnesses:

Lawrence Tighe, Henry Plunket, & Michael Unknown

- Margaret Tighe & Michael Forbes

  - Margaret Forbes – bapt. 17 Jun 1850 (Baptism, **St. Michan Parish (RC)**)

- Margaret Tighe & Patrick Graham

  - Jane Graham – bapt. 1849 (Baptism, **St. Mary Parish (RC)**)

- Margaret Tighe & Patrick Greckon

  - Mary Margaret Greckon – bapt. 1860 (Baptism, **St. Mary Parish (RC)**)

Hurst

- Margaret Tighe & Patrick Green – 14 Aug 1848 (Marriage, **St. Andrew Parish** (RC))

- Margaret Tighe & Patrick Grehan

    o James Grehan – bapt. 1865 (Baptism, **St. Mary Parish** (RC))

- Margaret Tighe & Patrick Grehan

    o Patrick Grehan & Elizabeth Keefe – 16 Apr 1878 (Marriage, **Harrington Street Parish** (RC))

Patrick Grehan (son):

Residence - 1 Montague Court - April 16, 1878

Elizabeth Keefe, daughter of Michael Keefe & Catherine Moran (daughter-in-law):

Residence - 1 Montague Place - April 16, 1878

    o Mary Grehan & Patrick Coogan – 17 Feb 1890 (Marriage, **Harrington Street Parish** (RC))

Mary Grehan (daughter):

Residence - 8 Montague Place - February 17, 1890

Patrick Coogan, son of William Coogan & Margaret Sherlock (son-in-law):

Residence - 8 Montague Place - February 17, 1890

    o Thomas Grehan & Catherine Byrne (B y r n e) – 24 Aug 1890 (Marriage, **Harrington Street Parish** (RC))

Thomas Grehan (son):

Residence - 18 Great Longford Street - August 24, 1890

Tighe Surname Ireland: 1600s to 1900s

Catherine Byrne, daughter of Daniel Byrne & Catherine McNally (daughter-in-law):

> Residence - 6 Wexford Street - August 24, 1890

- Margaret Tighe & Patrick O'Cregan

  - Owen O'Cregan – bapt. 1858 (Baptism, **St. Mary Parish** (RC))

- Margaret Tighe & Patrick Quigley – 20 Jan 1843 (Marriage, **St. James Parish** (RC))

- Margaret Tighe & Philip Whitty – 19 May 1834 (Marriage, **St. Michan Parish** (RC))

- Margaret Tighe & Sterne (S t e r n e) Phillips – 13 Sep 1823 (Marriage, **St. Peter Parish**)

Margaret Tighe (wife):

> Residence - St. Peter Parish - September 13, 1823

Sterne Phillips (husband):

> Residence - Athboy - September 13, 1823

Wedding Witness:

Sterne Tighe

- Margaret Tighe & Thomas Kane – 21 Apr 1808 (Marriage, **St. Andrew Parish** (RC))

- Margaret Tighe & William Sheehan

  - John Joseph Sheehan – b. 10 Jan 1899, bapt. 22 Jan 1899 (Baptism, **Rathmines Parish** (RC))

  - Madeline Bridget Sheehan – b. 21 Mar 1900, bapt. 27 Mar 1900 (Baptism, **Harrington Street Parish** (RC)) o Anne Martha Sheehan – b. 30 Jun 1901, bapt. 5 Jul 1901 (Baptism, **Harrington Street Parish** (RC))

William Sheehan (father):

Residence - 1 Shamwell Villa, Harold's Cross - January 22, 1899

11 Windsor Terrace - March 27, 1900

July 5, 1901

• Martha Tighe & James McCann – 22 Jun 1794 (Marriage, **St. Nicholas Parish** (RC))

Wedding Witnesses:

Matthew Lynch & Catherine Tighe

• Mary Tighe & Alexander Yeates

o Thomas Yeates – b. 30 Oct 1871, bapt. 10 Nov 1871 (Baptism, **St. Catherine Parish** (RC))

o Alexander Yeates – b. 29 Aug 1876, bapt. 4 Sep 1876 (Baptism, **St. Michan Parish** (RC))

o Patrick John Yeates – b. 18 Jul 1879, bapt. 25 Jul 1879 (Baptism, **St. Michan Parish** (RC))

o Robert Francis Yeates – b. 3 Feb 1884, bapt. 6 Feb 1884 (Baptism, **St. Michan Parish** (RC))

Alexander Yeates (father):

Residence - 5 Summer Street - November 10, 1871

25 Charles Street - September 4, 1876

July 25, 1879

February 6, 1884

Tighe Surname Ireland: 1600s to 1900s

- Mary Tighe & Andrew Barrett

  o Anne Barrett – b. 12 Jul 1878, bapt. 15 Jul 1878 (Baptism, **St. Nicholas Parish (RC)**)

Andrew Barrett (father):

Residence - 15 Dean Street - July 15, 1878

- Mary Tighe & Daniel McCarthy

  o Daniel McCarthy – bapt. 1 Apr 1838 (Baptism, **Drimoleague Parish (RC)**)

  o Ellen McCarthy – bapt. 21 Apr 1844 (Baptism, **Drimoleague Parish (RC)**)

- Mary Tighe & Edward Purcell – 11 Jan 1829 (Baptism, **Rathmines Parish (RC)**)

- Mary Tighe & Gulielmo Cruise

  o Robert Cruise – bapt. Jan 1817 (Baptism, **St. Nicholas Parish (RC)**)

- Mary Tighe & Henry Ash – 4 Feb 1743 (Marriage, **St. Michael Parish**)

- Mary Tighe & James Dunne

  o Patrick Dunne – bapt. 30 Aug 1789 (Baptism, **St. Catherine Parish (RC)**)

  o Mary Dunne – bapt. 27 Dec 1800 (Baptism, **St. Michan Parish (RC)**)

- Mary Tighe & James Gibney

  o Anne Gibney – bapt. 18 Sep 1782 (Baptism, **St. James Parish (RC)**)

  o Mary Gibney – bapt. 27 Apr 1787 (Baptism, **St. James Parish (RC)**)

- Mary Tighe & James Quinn

  o Hannah Quinn – bapt. 22 Feb 1805 (Baptism, **St. Michan Parish (RC)**)

- Mary Tighe & John Bray – 14 Feb 1834 (Marriage, **St. Nicholas Parish (RC)**)

  o Mary Bray – bapt. 3 Sep 1834 (Baptism, **St. Nicholas Parish (RC)**)

  o Anne Bray – bapt. 29 Oct 1838 (Baptism, **St. Nicholas Parish (RC)**)

Hurst

Wedding Witnesses:

John Trevors & Bridget Bray

- Mary Tighe & John Curtis – 23 Feb 1711 (Marriage, **St. Michan Parish**)

John Curtis (husband):

Occupation - Esquire - February 23, 1711

- Mary Tighe & John Hall
  - Elizabeth Hall – bapt. 1845 (Baptism, **Saggart Parish** (RC))

- Mary Tighe & John Kennedy
  - John Kennedy – b. 1866, bapt. 1866 (Baptism, **St. Mary Parish** (RC))

- Mary Tighe & John Kenny – 8 Sep 1862 (Marriage, **St. Mary Parish** (RC))
  - Alice Kenny – b. 1868, bapt. 1868 (Baptism, **St. Mary Parish** (RC))
  - Mary Anne Kenny – b. 1870, bapt. 1870 (Baptism, **St. Mary Parish** (RC))
  - Patrick Kenny – b. 1872, bapt. 1872 (Baptism, **St. Mary Parish** (RC))
  - Michael Kenny – b. 1874, bapt. 1874 (Baptism, **St. Mary Parish** (RC))
  - Patrick Kenny – b. 1876, bapt. 1876 (Baptism, **St. Mary Parish** (RC))
  - Gulielmo Kenny – b. 27 Aug 1878, bapt. 9 Sep 1878 (Baptism, **St. Mary, Haddington Road Parish** (RC))

John Kenny (father):

Residence - 2 Flemings Place - September 9, 1878

- Mary Tighe & John Quinn
  - Mary Jane Quinn – b. 17 Aug 1858, bapt. 20 Aug 1858 (Baptism, **St. Mary, Pro Cathedral Parish** (RC))

Tighe Surname Ireland: 1600s to 1900s

John Quinn (father):

Residence - 1 Nerney's Court - August 20, 1858

- Mary Tighe & John Smyth – 8 Dec 1820 (Marriage, **St. Mary, Pro Cathedral Parish** (RC))

- Mary Tighe & John P. Irwin – 9 May 1831 (Marriage, **St. Michan Parish** (RC))

  o Charles Irwin – b. 1844, bapt. 1844 (Baptism, **Rathfarnham Parish** (RC))

  o John Irwin – b. 1846, bapt. 1846 (Baptism, **Rathfarnham Parish** (RC))

  o William Irwin – b. 1847, bapt. 1847 (Baptism, **Rathfarnham Parish** (RC))

- Mary Tighe & Joseph Dalton

  o Joseph Dalton – b. 17 Jan 1883, bapt. 22 Jan 1883 (Baptism, **St. Mary, Pro Cathedral Parish** (RC))

Joseph Dalton (father):

Residence - 5 Talbot Street - January 22, 1883

- Mary Tighe & Joseph Sewell

  o Christopher Sewell – b. 24 Dec 1867, bapt. 30 Mar 1868 (Baptism, **St. Mary, Pro Cathedral Parish** (RC))

Joseph Sewell (father):

Residence - 61 Jervis Street - March 30, 1868

- Mary Tighe & Matthew Smullen – 14 Nov 1743 (Marriage, **St. Catherine Parish** (RC))

Wedding Witnesses:

Honor Delahunty & Patrick Smullen

Hurst

- Mary Tighe & Michael Flanagan

  ○ Bernard (B e r n a r d) Flanagan & Anne Hoggan – 21 Jul 1862 (Marriage, St. Lawrence Parish (RC))

Bernard Flanagan (son):

Residence - 12 Mayor Street - July 21, 1862

Anne Hoggan, daughter of Daniel Hoggan & Sarah McDermott (daughter-in-law):

Residence - 12 Mayor Street - July 21, 1862

Wedding Witnesses:

Daniel Bannon & Bridget Tighe

- Mary Tighe & Michael John William Griffin

  ○ Isabel Griffin & Patrick Edney – 8 Jul 1883 (Marriage, Harrington Street Parish (RC))

Isabel Griffin (daughter):

Residence - 21 Charlotte Street - July 8, 1883

Patrick Edney, son of John Edney & Mary Fitzsimmons (son-in-law):

Residence - 19 Charlemont Street - July 8, 1883

  ○ John Griffin – b. 6 Sep 1859, bapt. 12 Sep 1859 (Baptism, St. James Parish (RC))

  ○ Anne Griffin – b. 14 Jan 1861, bapt. 29 Jan 1861 (Baptism, SS. Michael & John Parish (RC))

  ○ Nicholas Joseph Griffin – bapt. 29 Jun 1868 (Baptism, St. Nicholas Parish (RC))

  ○ Patrick Griffin – b. 6 Aug 1869, bapt. 23 Aug 1869 (Baptism, St. Nicholas Parish (RC))

Tighe Surname Ireland: 1600s to 1900s

- o Henry Francis Griffin – b. 14 Sep 1871, bapt. 15 Sep 1871 (Baptism, **St. Nicholas Parish (RC)**)

- o Christopher Griffin – b. 1 Jan 1874, bapt. 2 Jan 1874 (Baptism, **St. Nicholas Parish (RC)**)

- o John Griffin – b. 5 Feb 1876, bapt. 18 Feb 1876 (Baptism, **St. Nicholas Parish (RC)**)

- o Elizabeth Griffin – b. 12 Dec 1877, bapt. 14 Dec 1877 (Baptism, **St. Nicholas Parish (RC)**)

Michael Griffin (father):

Residence - James Street - September 12, 1859

      57 George's Street - January 29, 1861

      1 Coombe - June 29, 1868

      12 Patrick's Close - August 23, 1869

      28 Hanover Lane - September 15, 1871

      16 Patrick Street - January 2, 1874

      3 Walker's Alley - February 18, 1876

      24 Plunket Street - December 14, 1877

- • Mary Tighe & Michael Irvine – 23 May 1814 (Marriage, **St. Peter Parish**)

Mary Tighe (wife):

Residence - St. Peter Parish - May 23, 1814

- • Mary Tighe & Patrick Ellis
  - o Jane Ellis – b. 18 Feb 1872, bapt. 8 Mar 1872 (Baptism, **St. Nicholas Parish (RC)**)

Hurst

Patrick Ellis (father):

Residence - 31 Peter Street - March 8, 1872

- Mary Tighe & Peter Hobson – 25 Dec 1765 (Marriage, **St. Catherine Parish (RC)**)

- Mary Tighe & Thomas Brown

  - Mary Brown – b. 1 Oct 1879, bapt. 13 Oct 1879 (Baptism, **St. Nicholas Parish (RC)**)

Thomas Brown (father):

Residence - 3 Bishop Court - October 13, 1879

- Mary Tighe & Thomas Tandy – 14 May 1802 (Marriage, **St. George Parish**)

Mary Tighe (wife):

Residence - St. George Parish - May 14, 1802

Thomas Tandy (husband):

Residence - Johnsbrook, Co. Meath - May 14, 1802

Occupation - Esquire - May 14, 1802

- Mary Tighe & William Cruise

  - Susan Cruise – bapt. 25 Sep 1814 (Baptism, **SS. Michael & John Parish (RC)**)

  - William Cruise – bapt. 1822 (Baptism, **St. Mary Parish (RC)**)

  - Mary Anne Cruise – bapt. 1824 (Baptism, **St. Mary Parish (RC)**)

  - Joseph Cruise – bapt. May 1832 (Baptism, **St. Catherine Parish (RC)**)

- Mary Tighe & William Davis

  - Joseph Davis – bapt. 19 Dec 1813 (Baptism, **SS. Michael & John Parish (RC)**)

Tighe Surname Ireland: 1600s to 1900s

- Mary Tighe & William McHugh

  o James McHugh – b. 28 Oct 1871, bapt. 9 Nov 1871 (Baptism, **SS. Michael & John Parish** (RC))

  o Mary Louise McHugh – b. 1873, bapt. 1873 (Baptism, **St. Andrew Parish** (RC))

William McHugh (father):

Residence - 9 Fishamble Street - November 9, 1871

8 Fleet Street - 1873

- Mary Agnes Tighe & Patrick Duffy – 24 Nov 1856 (Marriage, **Rathfarnham Parish** (RC))

  o Thomas Goodwin Duffy – b. 27 Jun 1859, bapt. 3 Jul 1859 (Baptism, **Rathmines Parish** (RC))

  o Margaret Bridget Duffy – b. 1863, bapt. 1863 (Baptism, **Rathfarnham Parish** (RC))

  o Catherine M. Duffy – b. 28 Aug 1868, bapt. 30 Aug 1868 (Baptism, **Rathmines Parish** (RC))

  o Anne Mary Duffy – b. 4 May 1870, bapt. 8 May 1870 (Baptism, **Rathmines Parish** (RC))

Patrick Duffy (father):

Residence - Parnell Place - July 3, 1859

Roundtown - 1863

Richmond Street - August 30, 1868

Richmond Bridewell - May 8, 1870

- Mary Anne Tighe & Bernard (B e r n a r d) Dwyer – 15 Jan 1838 (Marriage, **St. James Parish (RC)**)

  o Catherine Dwyer – bapt. 21 Apr 1841 (Baptism, **St. James Parish** (RC))

  o Thomas Dwyer – bapt. 13 Apr 1843 (Baptism, **St. James Parish** (RC))

  o Bernard (B e r n a r d) Dwyer – bapt. 9 Sep 1847 (Baptism, **St. James Parish** (RC))

  o Mary Anne Dwyer – bapt. 19 May 1851 (Baptism, **St. James Parish** (RC))

  o Mary Jane Dwyer – bapt. 24 Feb 1853 (Baptism, **St. James Parish** (RC))

- Mary Anne Tighe & Daniel Ralph – 30 Nov 1815 (Marriage, **St. Mary, Pro Cathedral Parish (RC)**)

  o Catherine Ralph – bapt. Apr 1819 (Baptism, **St. Catherine Parish** (RC))

- Mary Anne Tighe & James Campbell – 21 Nov 1842 (Marriage, **St. Thomas Parish**)

Signatures:

Wedding Witness:

Thomas Ayre

Signature:

- Mary Anne Tighe & Patrick Morrissey – Oct 1832 (Marriage, **St. Michan Parish** (RC))

Tighe Surname Ireland: 1600s to 1900s

- Mary Bridget Tighe & Christopher J. Lynch

  o Anne Mary Josephine Lynch – b. 25 Oct 1896, bapt. 29 Oct 1896 (Baptism, **St. Joseph Parish (RC)**)

  o Edward F. Lynch – b. 29 Sep 1898, bapt. 2 Oct 1898 (Baptism, **St. Joseph Parish** (RC))

  o Agnes Mary Lynch – b. 7 Sep 1900, bapt. 8 Sep 1900 (Baptism, **St. Joseph Parish** (RC))

Christopher Lynch (father):

Residence - Terenure House - October 29, 1896

Terenure Village - October 2, 1898

Harold's Cross Road - September 8, 1900

- Mary Jane Tighe & Lawrence O'Toole

  o Christopher James O'Toole – b. 1874, bapt. 1874 (Baptism, **St. Andrew Parish** (RC))

Lawrence O'Toole (father):

Residence - 3 Great Clarence Street - 1874

- Rachel Tighe & William O'Halloran

  o Bridget Ethel O'Halloran & Charles Thorpe – 24 Nov 1898 (Marriage, **St. Mary, Pro Cathedral Parish (RC)**)

Bridget Ethel O'Halloran (daughter):

Residence - 95 Marlborough Street - November 24, 1898

Charles Thorpe, son of Charles Thorpe & Mary Feller (son-in-law):

Residence - 16 North Strand - November 24, 1898

Hurst

- Rose Tighe & Philip Dunne – 17 Oct 1836 (Marriage, **St. Peter Parish**)

Rose Tighe (wife):

Residence - Stephen's Green, St. Peter Parish - October 17, 1836

Philip Dunne (husband):

Residence - Leeson Street, St. Peter Parish - October 17, 1836

- Rose Tighe & Thomas Pilon – 1 Jan 1807 (Marriage, **St. Audoen Parish (RC)**)

Wedding Witnesses:

Daniel Tighe & James Dawson

- Sarah Tighe & Gulielmo Kelly – 2 Aug 1841 (Marriage, **St. Nicholas Parish (RC)**)
- Sarah Tighe & Joseph Gardiner
    - Thomas Gardiner – b. 1859, bapt. 1859 (Baptism, **St. Andrew Parish (RC)**)

Joseph Gardiner (father):

Residence - 3 Lees Lane - 1859

- Sarah Tighe & Patrick Boland
    - Mary Elizabeth Boland – b. 14 Jan 1873, bapt. 7 Feb 1873 (Baptism, **St. Michan Parish (RC)**)

Patrick Boland (father):

Residence - 6 White's Lane - February 7, 1873

Tighe Surname Ireland: 1600s to 1900s

- Sarah Mary Tighe & John Quinn

  o Sarah Mary Quinn – b. 3 Mar 1879, bapt. 4 Mar 1879 (Baptism, **St. James Parish** (RC))

John Quinn (father):

Residence - Dolphin's Barn - March 4, 1879

- Sophie Tighe & James Gilligan

  o Peter Gilligan – bapt. 7 Dec 1851 (Baptism, **Rathmines Parish** (RC))

- Susan Tighe & Edward Haycock – 5 Sep 1829 (Marriage, **St. Catherine Parish** (RC))

  o Margaret Haycock – bapt. 20 Jun 1830 (Baptism, **St. Catherine Parish** (RC))

- Susan Tighe & James Duggan

  o Catherine Ellen Duggan – b. 1862, bapt. 1862 (Baptism, **St. Andrew Parish** (RC))

James Duggan (father):

Residence - 6 Molesworth Street - 1862

- Teresa Tighe & Edward Caffrey

  o Mary Esther Caffrey – b. 13 Apr 1895, bapt. 13 Apr 1895 (Baptism, **St. Mary, Pro Cathedral Parish** (RC))

  o Sarah Mary Caffrey – b. 28 May 1897, bapt. 28 May 1897 (Baptism, **St. Mary, Pro Cathedral Parish** (RC))

Edward Caffrey (father):

Residence - Rotunda Hospital - April 13, 1895

Rotunda - May 28, 1897

- Teresa Tighe & William Thomas Mullen

  o Margaret Mullen – b. 9 Jun 1806, bapt. 15 Jun 1806 (Baptism, **St. Catherine Parish** (RC))

  o Anne Mullen – bapt. 18 Feb 1810 (Baptism, **St. Catherine Parish** (RC))

  o Anne Mullen – bapt. 1 Nov 1811 (Baptism, **St. Catherine Parish** (RC))

  o Catherine Mullen – bapt. 8 Nov 1813 (Baptism, **St. Catherine Parish** (RC))

  o Michael Mullen – bapt. 5 Nov 1815 (Baptism, **St. Catherine Parish** (RC))

  o Mary Anne Mullen – bapt. 24 Aug 1817 (Baptism, **St. James Parish** (RC))

- Unknown Tighe & John Ussher – 27 Nov 1836 (Marriage, **St. Andrew Parish** (RC))

- Unknown Tighe & Thomas Lynch

  o Cecelia Lynch & John Fallon – 19 Jul 1865 (Marriage, **St. Mary, Pro Cathedral Parish** (RC))

Cecelia Lynch (daughter):

  Residence - Lavally - July 19, 1865

John Fallon, son of Bernard Fallon (son-in-law):

  Residence - 13 Reely Street - July 19, 1865

- Winifred Tighe & Archibald Crichton

  o Dennis Joseph Crichton – b. 15 Aug 1881, bapt. 24 Aug 1881 (Baptism, **St. Mary, Pro Cathedral Parish** (RC))

Archibald Crichton (father):

  Residence - 22 Capel Street - August 24, 1881

Tighe Surname Ireland: 1600s to 1900s

- Winifred Tighe & John Nealon

  o Esther Mary Nealon – b. 9 Apr 1879, bapt. 5 May 1879 (Baptism, **SS. Michael & John Parish (RC)**)

John Nealon (father):

Residence - 4 Longford Street - May 5, 1879

Name **V**ariations

Includes Latin and Abbreviated forms of names found in the original documents.

Abigail = Abigale, Abigall

Anne = Ann, Anna, Annae

Bartholomew = Barth, Bartholmeus, Bartholomeo

Bridget = Birgis, Brigid, Brigida, Bridgit

Catherine = Catharine, Catharina, Catharinae, Catherina, Cath, Catha, Cathae, Cathe, Cathn

Charles = Carolus, Charls, Chas

Christopher = Christoph

Daniel = Danielem, Danielis

Edmund = Edmond

Edward = Ed, Edwd

Eleanor = Eleo, Eleonora, Elinor, Ellenor

Elizabeth = Betty, Elisa, Elisabeth, Eliz, Eliza, Elizab, Elizh, Elizth

Ellen = Elena, Ellena

Emily = Emilia

Esther = Essie, Ester

Francis = Fransicum

George = Geo, Georg, Georgius

Grace = Gratiae

Gulielmo = Guil, Guillelmi, Gulielmum, Guillelmus, Gulmi

Helen = Helena

Honor = Hanora, Honora

James = Jacobi, Jacobus, Jas

Jane = Joanna

Jeanne = Jeannae, Joannae

Joan = Johanna, Joney

John = Jno, Joannem, Joannes, Johannis

Joseph = Jos

Juliana = Julian

Leticia = Letitia, Lettice, Letticia

Lewis = Louis

Luke = Lucas

Margaret = Margarita, Margaritae, Margeret, Marget, Margt

Martha = Marthae

Mary = Maria, My

Mary Anne = Marianna, Marianne, Maryanne

Michael = Michaelis, Michl

Patrick = Pat, Patt, Patk, Patricii, Patricius

Peter = Petri

Richard = Ricardi, Ricardus, Rich, Richd

Robert = Roberti

Rose = Rosa, Rosae

Thomas = Thom, Thomae, Thoms, Thos, Ths

Timothy = Timotheus, Timy

William = Wil, Will, Willm, Wm

Notes

Notes

Notes

Notes

Notes

Notes

Index

D

N

O

Tighe Surname Ireland: 1600s to 1900s

T

Hurst

1854 Jan 13 54
1855 Oct 17 45
1856 Nov 21 89
1861 Sep 8 41
1863 Sep 24 42
1879 Apr 13 37
1887 Aug 21 44
1889 Jan 23 8
John A.
 1870 Feb 22 34
John Atkinson
 1811 120
John Bernard (B e r n a r d)
 1857 Feb 25 33
John F.
 1856 Aug 140
John Francis Xavier
 1854 Nov 29 10
John Joseph
 1858 Feb 24 108
 1875 Nov 14 96
John Michael
 1865 Dec 15 28
John Patrick
 1877 Aug 17 52
 1877 Mar 2 22
Joseph
 1826 140
 1845 6
 1861 Jun 4 54
 1868 Jul 29 48
 1869 36
 1870 Oct 14 54
 1871 Jan 9 53
 1884 Oct 16 44
Joseph James
 1868 Aug 9 20
 1897 Feb 10 18
Joseph Stephen
 1871 Dec 26 34
Josephine Mary
 1873 62
Julie
 1863 Aug 141

Kathleen Christine
 1898 Dec 8 81
Margaret
 1815 141
 1851 Sep 8 71
 1857 Nov 20 12
 1884 82
 1897 Apr 27 81
Margaret Anne
 1877 Jul 25 12
Margaret Catherine
 1857 Jan 4 111
Margaret Frances
 1865 Nov 2 67
Margaret Mary
 1875 Jul 10 6
 1883 Aug 12 52
Martin
 1858 Apr 12 59
Mary
 1788 142
 1815 Apr 22 46
 1856 Apr 14 84
 1856 Apr 6 54
 1857 68
 1859 Dec 22 89
 1860 Apr 15 104
 1862 Jul 15 96
 1867 102
 1869 Nov 16 106
 1871 26
 1872 Dec 8 53
 1874 Jan 27 61
 1877 Aug 20 96
 1880 66
 1881 82
 1888 Feb 18 7
Mary Anne
 1862 Sep 13 36
 1866 Sep 6 48
 1870 19
 1873 Mar 1 5
 1876 Oct 4 35

Hurst

Tighe Surname Ireland: 1600s to 1900s

Hurst

About The Author

Donovan Hurst graduated from San Diego State University with a Bachelor of Arts in the major field of studies of History and a minor in the field of studies of Anthropology. He is a current member of The General Society of Mayflower Descendants and has been conducting genealogical research for over 10 years tracing back his ancestors to their ancestral homelands in Denmark, England, France, Germany, Ireland, Norway, and Scotland.

www.ingramcontent.com/pod-product-compliance
Lightning Source LLC
Chambersburg PA
CBHW080328270326
41927CB00014B/3134